I hope you enjoy learning more about Lorado Taft!

Lynn Allyn Young
October 2014

BEAUTIFUL DREAMER

BEAUTIFUL DREAMER:

The Completed Works
and Unfulfilled Plans
of Sculptor Lorado Taft

Lynn Allyn Young

I dedicate this book to Betty M.E. Croft,
whose love for Lorado Taft equals my own.
Without her unflagging support it never would have been completed.

I thank my mother, Josephine Eyestone Allyn, who gave me a love and appreciation for art in all its forms,
and my father, C. Vance Allyn, who shared with me his compulsion for research and puzzle-solving.

My appreciation goes out to Pat Talbot, whose continuing education field trips and lectures introduced
me to Lorado Taft when I was a volunteer docent with the Chicago Architecture Foundation,
and to Betty Benson, who knew Taft personally in the 1930s and kept an extraordinary collection of
clippings about him and shared them with me before giving them to the
Eagle's Nest Art Colony Collection in Oregon, Illinois.

My gratitude to Lewis Williams, Allen Weller, Robert LaFrance, and Timothy Garvey, whose research
and writings and apparent devotion to Taft helped me understand the sculptor in all his complexity.

And my boundless thanks to all the helpful people -- many of them
curious and interested reference librarians -- who have made the compilation of this book
so much easier; to Marsha Zaccone, director of the Oregon Public Library and the Eagle's Nest Art Colony
Collection, for all of her assistance; to good friends who provided motivation and insightful suggestions;
and to Jen Howard, whose editorial contributions were invaluable.

Cover and book design by Lynn Allyn Young. Cover image: plaster maquette of Lorado Taft's "The Blind"
on display in the Eagle's Nest Art Colony Collection, Oregon Public Library, Oregon, Illinois.

Publisher's Cataloging-in-Publication
(Provided by Quality Books, Inc.)

Young, Lynn Allyn.
    Beautiful dreamer : the completed works and
unfulfilled plans of sculptor Lorado Taft / Lynn Allyn
Young.
    p. cm.
Includes bibliographical references.
    ISBN 978-0-615-65632-8   1. Taft, Lorado, 1860-1936.
2. Sculptors--United States--Biography. 3. Sculpture,
American--20th century.   I. Taft, Lorado, 1860-1936. II. Title.

    NB237.T3Y68 2012   730.92

            QBI12-600153

TABLE OF CONTENTS

Introduction... ix
     "Spirit of Art" (1936-37)

The Earliest Years.. 1

Teaching and Lecturing.. 5
     "Solitude of the Soul" (1914)
     "Knowledge" (1902) and "Despair" (1898)
     Lorado Taft and the Cliff Dwellers Club

Portraiture 12
     Henry Hardin Cherry (1934)
     Charles H. Hackley ("Alma Mater") (1929)
     Thomas D. Gilbert (1895)
     Charles Page (1930)
     "Dreams and Death Masks"
     Various busts

Frances Willard.. 18
     Willard medallion (1898)
     Willard bust (Northwestern) (1898)
     Willard bust (Hall of Fame) 1923
     Willard bust (WCTU Library) (1931)
     Willard plaque (Indianapolis) (1929)

War Memorials.. 20
     Mt. Carroll (1891)
     Winchester (1892) & Oregon (1916)
     Gettysburg (1889)
     Vicksburg (1911)
     "Victory" (Danville) (1922)
     Omaha and Albany memorials
     "Defense of the Flag"
       Chickamauga, Ga. (1894)
       Jackson, Mich. (1904)
       Marion, Ind. (1915)

Grave Memorials 24
     "Eternal Silence" (Dexter Graves) (1909)
     "Crusader" (Victor Lawson) (1931)
     "Recording Angel" (Mrs. Clarence Shaler) (1923)
     William A. Foote Memorial (1923)

Columbian Exposition..26
    Horticulture Building designs
    Garfield Park: "Idyll" and "Pastoral" (1913)

Fountains...30
    Lafayette (1886)
    Ferguson Fountain of the Great Lakes (1913)
    Trotter Fountain (1911)
    Columbus Fountain (1912)
    Thatcher Fountain (1918)
    "Fish Boys" Fountain (1920s)

Abraham Lincoln, Stephen Douglas, and other historical figures.........39
    Douglas plaques (1901 and 1913)
    "Lincoln, the Young Lawyer" (1927)
    Lincoln statue in Lincoln's tomb
    Schuyler Colfax (1887)
    Ulysses S. Grant (1889)
    George Washington (1909)
    Annie Louise Keller (1929)

Low-relief Panels 45
    Bobs Roberts (1931)
    Katherine Lucinda Sharp (1921)
    Iroquois Theater (1910)
    Jonathan Prentiss Dolliver (1925)

Medals...48
    James Whitcomb Riley (1916)
    Medallic Art Society War Medal (1930)
    Medallic Art Society Great Lakes Medal (1930)

Midway Studios and previous studio locations 49

The Gates of Paradise...52

Dream Museum & Peep Shows..53

Eagle's Nest Colony..56
    Discovery of Taft's original studio

"Eternal Indian" and other Native Americans 58
    "Eternal Indian" (1911)
    New Black Hawk Center bronze (2005)
    Chief Paduke (1909)

Plan for Chicago's Midway Plaisance...63
    Midway Plan (1908)
    "Fountain of Creation"

"Fountain of Time" (1922) 67

The Elmwood "Pioneers" (1927) 76

"Alma Mater" (1929) 78

Chicago's Century of Progress 82
    "Justice" (1933)
    "Come Unto Me" (1933)

Louisiana's State Capitol (1933) 84

Nearing the end... 87
    Lincoln-Douglas debate monument and plaster model (1936)
    Don Carlos Taft bust (1936)
    Washington, Solomon & Morris & "Lady Liberty" panel (1941)

Krannert Art Museum exhibition.. 90

"The Blind" 91
    Oregon, Illinois maquette (1907)
    "Blind" tableau vivant (2007)
    Bronze figure grouping at Krannert Art Museum (1988)

"Orpheus Consoled" remains! (1922) 93

Mysteries solved: Mary Ella McGinnis (1888) 94

Pieces we can't see: "Mother & Child" (1914) 94

And new discoveries: "Aspiration" (1936) 95

Exciting plans for the future 96

Taft's death and gravesite.. 97

So where does Taft stand in the ranks of sculptors? 97

Endnotes 100

Photo Credits.. 109

Appendix A: Address at Lorado Taft funeral 114
Appendix B: Allen Weller obituary 117
Appendix C: Lewis Williams obituary 119
Appendix D: Chart of Taft works.. 120

MCMXXXVI

THE SPIRIT OF ART
DESIGN FOR THE ARCHE'S LIBRARY LORADO TAFT

Introduction

I first saw Lorado Taft's "Fountain of Time" in the early 1990s. I had just moved to Chicago. It was dirty, cracked, and neglected, but I was overwhelmed by the power of its figures. What kind of artist would create such a magnificent piece, and why was it being treated so poorly? I watched with great joy as a meticulous restoration gave it back its dignity.

As I absorbed more details about Chicago's history, I learned how much influence Taft had had over the city's public art in the early 1900s. He was indeed the "art missionary" of the Midwest, lecturing widely and pressing the point that sculpture adds civility to a developing culture. How I wish I could have heard him speak!

I started developing a list of Taft's sculptures, and then photographed as many as I could find in the Chicago area. For the most part they were being treated well, although few people I spoke with recognized Taft's name -- including students working in what had been his largest studio. I traveled wider afield, finding more and more pieces. Farther and farther I drove, and each piece I found was consistent in its craftsmanship. Even the pieces at Gettysburg, despite Taft's claims that they were less significant, told a story through their design. As I crossed off the locations on my list, the body of work that Taft created -- that still existed and was well preserved -- became overwhelming. Why wasn't his name still on people's lips?

Well, it turns out that the name of Taft is still alive and well in the little city of Oregon, Ill. Taft and his colleagues had spent many summers at an artists' colony next to the Rock River, and many of their works are still on display in a special exhibit hall atop the public library -- including a delicate plaster model of "The Blind," one of Taft's more complicated and impressive designs. Taft had erected an impressive 48-foot-tall statue of an Indian on a bluff overlooking the Rock River and, in addition, had designed a war memorial for the courthouse square and a small fountain for the city park. Lest Taft's name be forgotten in spite of his ongoing presence there, a retired librarian by the name of Betty M.E. Croft took it upon herself to make sure he was remembered. She defined a local "Sculpture Trail" that visitors could follow to see Taft's works and those of other local sculptors. She greeted travelers at the base of the "Eternal Indian" statue and provided them with information about Taft. And she convinced Oregon residents to participate in a tableau vivant of

(Facing page) "The Spirit of Art" has traveled one of the most circuitous routes to being viewed once again. Originally designed for the Arché Club, a Chicago women's organization dedicated to the arts, civics, and philanthropy, it ended up in the Midway Studios. When the studios were readied for student use, the panel went to the Krannert Art Museum, and it is now on display in a small gallery. One of Taft's last designs (1936-37), this relief was completed and cast in bronze by the sculptor's studio associates Fred Torrey and Mary Webster.

"The Blind" for its 100th anniversary. To celebrate Taft's 150th birthday in 2010, she ramped up her public relations efforts to reach as many people as possible.

The University of Illinois campus at Urbana-Champaign provides another "bastion" of Taft supporters. Taft's connection to the university, the presence of his family's home and the naming of a drive after him, the magnificent collection of his work protected by the Krannert Art Museum, and the statue of the "Alma Mater" that is familiar to all graduates -- these all help to keep his memory alive.

And then there's Taft's birthplace of Elmwood, Ill., where the residents respectfully maintain his gravesite and look with pride at his statue of "The Pioneers" in the town's central park. The town also is home to the Elmwood Historical Society and Lorado Taft Museum.

As I have taken picture after picture and assembled the scattered stories of Taft's life, the response has been: "I had no idea...." And that's the problem. Taft's works are spread far enough apart that, without his dynamic presence, his impact has been diluted. So this book is my attempt to impress readers with the depth and breadth of Taft's creativity. I hope it works!

In the meantime, I have created a website, http://www.taftbeautifuldreamer.com. On it I will be posting new Taft developments. In addition, I hope to encourage a dialogue with people from all over the world who have encountered one or more of Taft's works and would like to comment and share their photos. I encourage links to other sites that include photographs or articles relating to Taft. It would be exciting if works from Lewis Williams' dissertation list that I have been unable to locate come to the surface. Just as I have brought together this collection of Taft's works, I hope this website assembles a community of Taft followers that is larger than anyone can imagine. Please keep in touch!

-- Lynn Allyn Young

"We Americans think of art as pretty and amusing, but after all a superficial matter. It should be a part of our religion. There is a holiness in beauty as well as a 'beauty of holiness.' It ennobles life and helps to explain it. One thing which separates us from our brother animals is the fact that we can send messages down through the generations. We can send greetings to a world unborn. Conversely we can think back through the ages and be grateful to those who have wrought for us. The means by which this is done is art. Through poetry and painting and sculpture life begins to explain itself."[1]

– Lorado Taft

The Earliest Years

Lorado Taft was an Illinois native, born and raised. His father, Don Carlos, was born in 1827 in Swanzey, N.H., then graduated from Amherst College in Massachusetts in 1852 and the Union Theological Seminary in New York City in 1855, and was ordained in 1855.[2] In 1856 Don Carlos moved to Elmwood, Ill., to be headmaster of the newly established Elmwood Academy and also to be a part-time minister at the Congregational Church in which the academy was housed. One year later he married Mary Lucy Foster; they built a home on East Cypress Street in Elmwood.

Lorado Zadoc Taft was the first of four children, born April 29, 1860. Taft's middle name, Zadoc, was Don Carlos's father's first name, and Lorado stopped using it as soon as he was old enough to choose.[3] Even the name "Lorado" was shortened: The family called him "Rado," or "Roddy."[4]

Taft's second wife Ada Bartlett wrote of the little town where he grew up in a biography entitled *Lorado Taft: Sculptor and Citizen.* "[It] was settled by New Englanders, liberal in their culture but intolerant in their religion. They soon found that Mr. Taft's sermons were too liberal, with the consequence that teaching geology became his main work."[5] After Taft's brother, Florizel, was born in 1862, the family left Elmwood and Don Carlos became the principal of Metamora High School, a position he held until 1868. The family then moved to Minonk, where Don Carlos became principal of that high school. Two additional children were born: daughters Zulime in 1868 and Turbia Doctoria in 1870.

Taft's birthplace in Elmwood, Ill., was demolished, but its location is identified with a granite marker.

In 1871 Don Carlos became an assistant professor of geology at the newly founded Illinois Industrial University in Champaign, Ill. The following year he was named professor of geology and zoology at the university — a position he held until 1882 — and the family moved to Champaign and built a house one block from the campus.[6] (It was said that Don Carlos could have taught any subject in the curriculum.)[7]

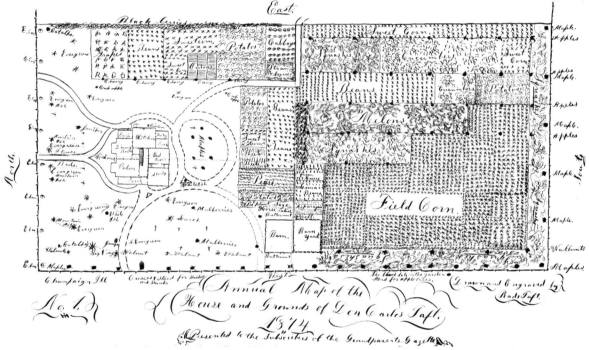

The Taft home in Champaign (photographed in 1940) and a map of the property drawn by Taft when he was 14

The university's regent, John Gregory, had bought a large collection of casts of Greek and Roman sculpture from Paris in 1874 with which to open the school's first art gallery. But shipping caused major damage to the pieces, and Taft wrote:

> *"Many were sadly injured; some were reduced to heaps of rubbish. With grim determination [Gregory] and my father set themselves to the almost hopeless task of assembling these fragments. This is where the boy comes in; to me it was a game as delightful as jig-saw puzzles. I was able to spy out hopeful splinters and locate chips much faster than could the bespectacled elders!"[8]*

Gregory located James Kenis, a journeyman sculptor from Belgium who was working in Chicago, to supervise restoration of the pieces. "I attached myself [to this] little Belgian sculptor like a stray dog," Taft wrote.[9] Taft's interest in art was sealed through this experience, and throughout the rest of his life he dreamed of assembling his own museum of ancient sculpture and architecture.

The university gallery opened in 1875 in University Hall, and the *Chicago Tribune* reported, "This grand collection of art is now the largest west of New York."[10] The first catalog of the gallery listed more than 900 objects, all copies of celebrated works in European museums.[11]

The Illinois Industrial University Art Gallery, from 1875

Kenis stayed on as instructor in clay modeling and architectural ornamentation; he taught the teenage Taft drawing, modeling, and sculpting until he left Champaign in 1877, at which point Taft took over as art instructor.[12]

Taft entered the university at 15 and graduated with a bachelor's degree in 1879 at the age of 19.[13] He wanted to study art in Paris, but his parents felt he was still too young to live abroad, so he stayed in Champaign and earned a master's degree a year later. In his master's thesis, "The English Language of the Twentieth Century: A Prediction," he claimed that spelling reform was needed; he presented his own system and gave reasons for each suggestion, then went on to use his simplified spelling in letters for nearly 20 years.[14]

Taft's parents finally allowed him to move to France. (Taft biographer Allen Weller compiled Taft's letters home into a fascinating book entitled *Lorado in Paris: The Letters of Lorado Taft 1880-1885.*[15]) He was immediately accepted to the prestigious École Nationale et Spéciale des Beaux-Arts in Paris. (Even renowned sculptor Auguste Rodin was refused entrance three times before getting in.)[16] Paris was the center of the art world at that time, and the highly competitive École provided a solid education in Greek and Roman art and a sharp focus on the nude model. Taft had learned German and French in his college years and adjusted quickly to the new Parisian environment. He studied with Augustin Dumont, Jean-Marie Bonnassieux, and Jules Thomas, among other prominent artists.[17] He received a number of prizes and honors during his stay, and three of his works in two different years were accepted for the Paris Salon, where they were seen along with hundreds of other examples of academic style.[18] He even sold some of his work, much to his great delight. Throughout his time in Paris he followed a rigorous schedule that included regular study visits to the Louvre. "I have always quietly expected to be somebody, a prize for which we must toil," he wrote.[19]

On Taft's first Sunday in Paris he attended services at the American Chapel, and soon he was teaching a Sunday school class there. He met an English clergyman, R.W. McAll, who had established a mission to the working classes in France, and he began working as a volunteer, teaching classes in English and organizing and presenting talks of all kinds to the "working people of the poorest and worst smelling class."[20]

In 1883, when his formal training was completed, Taft came back to Champaign for a year before returning to Paris. In addition to teaching French at the university and presenting several talks, he coordinated an art exhibition and showed 14 of his works, including portraits, sketches, and "ideal compositions."[21] Once back in Paris, he moved into a house vacated by American friends and a studio offered to him by the American sculptor H.H. Kitson. He started working with a passion. "There are no end of subjects," he wrote home.[22] He became acquainted with Simeon B. Williams, a real estate magnate who was to become his benefactor,

Lorado Taft (front, left) and his Paris art colleagues

providing him with introductions and financial support.[23] He returned to the McAll Mission and this time he was paid to present lectures, three or four nights a week, all around the city. His career as a professional lecturer had begun.[24]

Taft's letters don't say why he chose to leave Paris a second time and return to Illinois for good. It could have been the small amount of money he made selling his work; perhaps it was the prospect of an important commission; or it might have been the fact that he had met an interesting American woman in Paris, Carrie Scales, and she had returned to the States.[25] After a short stay in St. Louis, where he and Carrie became engaged, he settled in Chicago in January of 1886. Ada Bartlett Taft explained:

> *"He had long before decided to settle in Chicago, partly because he had grown up under the shadow and glamour of the great city of his state, but mainly because it was not overcrowded with sculptors and there was little competition and none of the fighting over opportunities as in New York. Alas, there were few opportunities to fight over, for Chicago did not feel any great need for statues. Art had not yet 'begun to hum' as one of the pioneer citizens is credited with prophesying it would in time. Indeed, when the interest did come, people distrusted home products, and were inclined to go straight to New York or to Europe where others had already laid the stamp of approval."[26]*

Taft and Carrie were married in 1890 and lived with Carrie's mother in Evanston, Ill., but Carrie died in childbirth in 1891. In 1896 Taft married Ada Bartlett. Ada was Carrie's cousin (her grandmother was Carrie's mother), and Taft had known her nearly as long as he had Carrie.[27] Their first home was in Chicago in the Hyde Park Hotel, and they lived in a number of apartments before buying a home.[28] They had three daughters: Emily (Douglas [Illinois congresswoman]), Mary (Smith), and Jessie Louise (Crane).

Teaching and Lecturing

In the fall of 1886 Taft took a position as instructor and head of the sculpture department in the new art school of the Art Institute in Chicago.[29] "I soon discovered that no one wanted my work but, strangely enough, the women's clubs liked to hear talk about sculpture!" he exclaimed.[30] However, when the Art Institute's new building was opened with a gala exhibition, the show contained four of his serious works.[31] The University of Chicago also hired him with the vaguely defined (and nontenured) title of "Professorial Lecturer on the History of Art." (Taft declared that he considered himself "in some sort 'Sculptor to the University of Chicago.'")[32]

Ada wrote:

> "The following analysis of Lorado's gift of speaking was written by the director of a Chautauqua association: 'Last night I had the pleasure of hearing Lorado Taft speak. He made such an impression as few men can make – an impression that would seem to be abiding. As you can well understand, I am rather a jaded listener, but there was something so different about Mr. Taft's address that I listened as though I were hearing a lecture for the first time. What a unique place he fills! The consummate skill and grace and simplicity and sincerity that characterize his work as a sculptor pervade his speaking…. There is much more that I observe, and by which I am impressed, but by nothing so much as the charming manner of the speaker, his artistic selection of matter and most of all his vital spiritual power….'"[33]

In 1899 Taft was offered a professorship at Vassar College but turned it down to stay in Chicago. "I believe I am in my own field right here," he responded. "I believe I am needed here…. I want my work to come out of the west, and if there is any glory in it, I want to share it with my own home people."[34]

A modeling class in Taft's studio. Taft is standing directly behind the nude model.

"Solitude of the Soul," completed in 1914, in its present Sculpture Court location (facing page), and in its original location next to Michelangelo's "Slave" (left) (from a vintage postcard)

By the early 1890s, Taft was receiving so many lecture requests that he had to send others in his place.[35] He remained associated with the Art Institute for 21 years as a studio teacher and longer as a lecturer. He relinquished his teaching position in the spring of 1907.[36] Interestingly, considering the length of time he spent at the Chicago Art Institute, only one of his works is now on display inside its museum. "Solitude of the Soul" (designed and exhibited by 1901 but not carved in marble until 1914) sits in the Roger McCormick Memorial Sculpture Court. It won a gold medal at the 1904 Louisiana Purchase Exposition,[37] and one critic called it "the first important example of his renaissance, larger, maturer in feeling."[38] It was agreed that this was Taft's first group to bring him national attention, and announced a new direction in his work and in his place in American art.[39] Yet *The Essential Guide to the Art Institute of Chicago* fails to mention Taft or this piece.[40]

In 1903 Taft produced his first book on American sculpture, *History of American Sculpture*, the pioneering work in its field.[41] Updated versions of this text in 1924, 1925, and 1930 were to remain the standard reference on this subject until Wayne Craven published *Sculpture in America* in 1968.[42]

Taft became a noted art authority, published in newspapers and magazines. He lectured all over the country – except Florida. Ada wrote, "He sometimes wondered whimsically 'how they ever got along without me in Florida.'"[43] His most popular lecture was a "clay talk," in which he modeled before the audience the head of a woman who changed from glamorous youth and beauty to haggard and shrunken old age.[44] He is said to have given this presentation some 1500 times.[45]

(Above) Taft poses with the head of a woman that he used for his "Clay Talks."

(Right) Among the pieces he brought to his lectures were "Knowledge" (1902) (far right) and "Despair" (1898) (near right), now displayed under plexiglas at the Art Museum in Rockford, Ill.

In the 1920s Taft began giving a free Sunday lecture at the Art Institute on the history of sculpture. Lewis Williams II described these presentations in his doctoral dissertation:

> "He is a fascinating lecturer, and under the spell of his words the vast field of sculpture becomes of vital interest to each member of his audience. The Art Institute never had more crowded halls than when he spoke. This became apparent when he gave his series of free talks at the institute, 1919-29. First Mr. Taft spoke in the clubroom where 54 lectures were delivered to over 13,000 listeners. The capacity of this hall soon was outgrown, and from 1921-29 Mr. Taft talked to crowded audiences in Fullerton hall. Here 186 free lectures were given to over 92,000 people, a record attendance mark, signifying an average audience of 490 in a hall that seats only 484."[46]

Ada added:

> "Dr. Harshe, Director of the Art Institute, wrote to him: 'It is always a matter of wonder to me how year after year, in these wonderful lectures of yours, you have been able to draw crowds of such magnitude, who exhibit the most intense interest in what you have to say. You either do not repeat yourself, or the groups of listeners are all different, or you exert a special kind of magic to which you only have the key. The Art Institute would not be the same institution without the Lorado Taft lectures.'"[47]

In 1921, Taft published *Modern Tendencies in Sculpture*, a compilation of his Art Institute lectures.[48] This book continues to be regarded as an excellent survey of American sculpture in the early years of the 20th century; it offered a distinct perspective on the development of European sculpture scene at that time.[49]

As he continued to lecture, he also conducted tours to view his favorite sculptures. For many summers, beginning in 1906, he led groups through buildings and museums through the auspices of the Bureau of University Travel.[50]

In 1918 the YMCA invited him to travel to France to lecture to American soldiers on the beauties of the French cathedrals. The job expanded to include a unique American Expeditionary Forces University, where troops waiting shipment home could study subjects of their choice. Taft wrote that his lectures were well received. On Feb. 19 he wrote, "I had my reward, for the audience, not large but select, almost mobbed me afterwards and overwhelmed me with compliments. It's fun to take an indifferent crowd and bring it to terms."[51] Taft often spoke at the University of Illinois, his alma mater, and in 1919 he was named as "non-resident Professor of Art." The school established a lecture fund (which still exists) to bring him to the campus each spring for a series of lectures.[52] Taft biographer Allen Weller wrote that Taft was "probably the only person who attracted standing-room-only audiences to lectures on art in the University Auditorium."[53]

Taft became a member of numerous societies and participated in several prominent art clubs and organizations. During the mid-1920s, he was an active member of more than 30 art and civic organizations including, among the more important, the American Federation of Arts, the National Academy of Design, the National Sculpture Society, the Bureau of University Travel, and the American Civic Association.[54]

1932 University Travel brochure advertising a Taft tour to Europe

In a vintage photo of Cliff Dwellers Club members from May 3, 1920, Taft is shown in the front center, along with (clockwise from Taft's left) William O. Goodman (a lumberman and founder of the Goodman Theatre), George Eggers (art professor), George Ganierre (artist), Howard Van Doren Shaw (architect), Leonard Crunelle (sculptor), E.O. Grover (author), Clarence Hough (author), Albin Polasek (sculptor), and Louis Sullivan (architect).

Of the many cultural organizations Taft joined, the Cliff Dwellers Club appears to have had a personal significance for him, although archival references to his membership are few. After the exhilarating work at the 1893 Columbian Exposition was completed and the participating artists left Chicago, he missed the camaraderie and opportunities to share ideas. His studio on Van Buren Street became a gathering place for rising young artists and writers of Chicago, and they took the name "The Little Room."

Writer Hamlin Garland came to Chicago in 1892, predicting that the city "was about to take its place as one of the literary capitals of the world." Soon after his arrival, he was invited to give a lecture on "Impressionism in Art," and he met Taft following his presentation. This, writes Cliff Dwellers archivist Henry Regnery, "was the beginning of a long and fruitful friendship, one result of which was Garland's marriage in 1899 to Taft's sister, Zulime."[55] Garland shared his impression of Taft in his novel, *Daughter of the Middle Border*:

> *"Taft was especially witty in his sly, sideways comment, and often when several of us were in hot debate, his sententious or humorous retorts cut or stung in the defense of some aesthetic principle much more effectively than most of my harangues. Sculpture with him was a religious faith, and he defended it manfully and practised it with skill and industry which was astounding...."[56]*

Garland was the person who came up with the idea to form what became known as the Cliff Dwellers Club, and he approached Taft with the suggestion. Regnery writes:

> *"'The time has come,' he remarked to his brother-in-law Lorado Taft, 'when a successful literary and artistic club can be established and maintained.' What he had in mind was a club which would be like the Players in New York, 'a meeting place for artists and writers, a rallying point for Midland Arts.' Besides Taft, Garland discussed the idea with other friends from the Little Room, including Henry Fuller, Charles Francis Browne, and Ralph Clarkson. All thought well of the idea except his good friend, Henry B. Fuller, whose novel,* The Cliff-Dwellers, *is said to have provided the name for the new club."[57]*

The new club was formally organized at a meeting on November 6, 1907. A constitution was adopted that provided that the membership be limited to 250, of whom three-fifths "shall be professionally engaged in literature, painting, sculpture, architecture, music, or drama, and two-fifths shall be lay members comprising persons who are connoisseurs and lovers of the fine arts."[58] Taft was one of the first directors and, in the first few years, also served on the art and reception committees. He was listed as a member every year until 1935 and then as an honorary member for one year until his death.

The group leased the penthouse of Chicago's Orchestra Hall on Michigan Avenue, and Howard Van Doren Shaw designed the interior, called the "kiva," complete with a large fireplace, grand piano, and space for an art gallery.[59] The room was inaugurated on January 6, 1909, and, as author and University of Chicago professor Robert Herrick told the group in attendance:

> "'The opening of this club has very real significance for the community of Chicago. It means that those of us who are engaged in the practice of the arts, who are interested in the expression of our national life in something other than material accomplishments and mere efficiency, are to have a home. Here refugees from small-town bourgeois and urban nouveau-riche philistines alike could befriend each other and practice the evanescent art of conversation.'"[60]

The dining room would have many configurations throughout the years, but one member, Dudley Crafts Watson, described the days "when writers, painters, musicians and others sat at a round table in the middle of the dining room until its sixteen places were filled."[61]

Several chairs are yet to be occupied around the fabled round table at the Cliff Dwellers Club in this photo from March of 1912. Taft is third from left, along with fellow artists Ralph Clarkson, Charles Mulligan, Wilson Irvine, C.F. Browne, W.H. Tuttle, and two men who are unidentified.

Taft would be pleased to know that the Cliff Dwellers Club is still going strong more than 100 years later. Despite loud public protest, it moved to a new location atop the Borg-Warner Building in 1996. Chicago architect Larry Booth designed the new space and made sure the historic fireplace was moved intact. It continues to invite those professionally involved with the arts -- from literature, painting, music, architecture, sculpture or any of the allied arts -- or who appreciate the arts to consider becoming a member.[62] Sculptors are especially welcome.

Portraiture

Establishing a name for himself as a sculptor when he first moved to Chicago from Paris turned out to be a slower process than Taft expected. One of his assistants, Trygve Rovelstad, wrote that at first Taft sold copies or statuettes of famous sculpture to people who could not afford the originals.[63] He modeled decorative trim, firebacks, and grates for the Harris Iron Works and other companies.[64]

The first paying job he received in the city was for "$50.00 worth of sculpture in butter" for a YMCA dairy festival. Bo Peep, a butter cow, and a dairymaid – labeled "Maid in Butter" – were, he wrote home, "well received, a big success."[65] In 1890 he was paid $35 per day and expenses to travel to Detroit and create a butter sculpture of Captain Moore, director of the Masonic Fair.[66]

Taft's skill with portraiture, developed at the École, helped solidify his reputation outside of the lecture arena. In the course of his lifetime he created hundreds of busts, relief portraits, and monuments that recorded the personalities and appearance of America's leaders in political, intellectual, and artistic life.

Clockwise from top left, the memorial to Charles Hackley, entitled "Alma Mater," on the campus of the Muskegon (Mich.) High School (1929); Thomas D. Gilbert, Veterans Memorial Park, Grand Rapids, Mich. (1895); and the Charles Page Memorial (1930) in Page Memorial Park, Sand Springs, Okla.

(Facing page) The Henry Hardin Cherry sculpture (1934) at the entrance to Cherry Hall, Western Kentucky University, Bowling Green, Ky.

Taft wasn't particularly happy sculpting portraits. He found many of the commissions to be "mundane -- even degrading" when, as was often the case, it required the artist to base his work on death masks. So often was he called to deathbeds, Taft later complained, he had begun to feel like "a Siberian convict chained to a corpse."[67] He wrote sadly that creating death masks and soldier statues for war monuments was not the profession which he thought he had chosen.[68]

Dreams and Death Masks
The Chicago Record, Tuesday, June 6, 1899, page 4

I am tired of dead folk. I am tired of living on them.

Our busy people have no time to pose for their portraits while they are alive, but after the scramble is over they are glad enough to while away their leisure in a studio. I have a delightful "morgue" lined with death masks and still deader busts. My shop is a resort of ghosts of all degrees. I come in unexpectedly and find it full of excellent spirits. That is where we differ – my studio and I. The more they revel the more I am depressed. It is a ghoulish way to live. For twelve years I have felt like a Siberian convict chained to a corpse.

They have an eternity on their hands – these quiet, undemonstrative people – but the artist has not. What he could do well from life in a few hours' time he does badly with weeks of toil from the poor data furnished him. A ghastly mask, a retouched photograph or two and a necktie may be all that is left, but a "speaking likeness" is required.

Referring to the proposed Dewey memorial, several of the newspapers agree that a man should have no monument during his lifetime. They speak as though this were an axiom of the art. Of course it is well to guard against possible slips in grace and to bear in mind that the hero of the hour is human and fallible. The greatest of men might get drunk inopportunely, or embezzle, or run away with his typewriter. It may not be likely, but such things have happened, and it is always safer to be dead. But if you are reasonably certain that you want to honor a man with a statue or a bust, do, I beg of you, give the sculptor a chance at him while he is alive. Wrap the model up afterward and put it in a safety vault, if you will, and wait. But make sure of getting the live man into the bronze or marble. We cannot make great, living works out of "remains." A plausible, conventional effigy is the best that even a good sculptor can do, if he has not the individual to look at. His figure may be vastly better looking than the subject ever was, but it is personality that we want in portraiture. A sketch by Hans Holbein is worth a score of Cabanels.

Let me tell you a story of dreams and death masks. It sounds rather gruesome, but in reality it is funny. An Illinois boy of 13 chose the profession of sculptor. For some reason his parents encouraged this ambition. He has never understood why otherwise practical people should have done so. Evidently there was a screw loose somewhere, for which he is still devoutly grateful. There was nothing remarkable about the boy excepting his love of beauty and his horror of death. He would go a block out of his way to avoid passing the undertaker's shop, and he would go still farther any day for the privilege of looking at a pretty face. When he was 15 years old some one gave him a life of Thorwaldsen, full of pictures of dainty reliefs and graceful statues. He read the book and pored over the cuts enthusiastically but critically, never doubting his own ability to do as well. He did not doubt, either, that all the United States was waiting with infinite desire for his fair nymphs and heroes, his Danaids and Graces and Mercurys and Apollos, as did Europe for the works of the great Danish sculptor. Youth is very confident – and he was only 15, you know.

He read the story of Thorwaldsen's return to his native land and of the great fete with which he was welcomed, and his cheeks burned as in boyish imagination he saw himself welcomed back to America by leading citizens of New York and Chicago, Champaign and Urbana. He could almost hear the bands playing as he fell asleep o'nights, and he saw himself bowing with modest dignity to the hysterical crowds on either side of his triumphal coach. These things were evanescent and fled with the dew of early years. The goddesses and heroes persisted. He dreamed of them constantly and had great white visions of wonderful groups and beliefs. He slept soundly and the nymphs were always of marble or plaster.

Back from Paris and established in a great city, the country boy was a country boy still. He had given up the welcome and the brass bands and hoarse huzzas and the flags many years before, but the fair visions remained. Some had grown a little wan and indistinct, but others he knew by heart. He lived in a world of lovely, intangible beings with radiant, half-veiled faces, who beckoned to him and smiled encouragement. Surely these strange hurrying people of the street must want his wares. They would soon be crowding his studio and disputing for his rare creations. He would not sell to the first comer, not he! His figures would be his living companions, children of his fancy, and he would not "bind them out" as though they were orphans in unsympathetic households. Those to whom he intrusted his marble treasures must not only keep them clean and in a good light, but must understand and love them as he had. Furthermore, he must be permitted to visit them from time to time to see how they were doing. These essential preliminaries being arranged, he would ask a trifle of $10,000 or $15,000 for each, not so much in way of payment as a guaranty of good faith. Yes, most assuredly he was a country boy still; five years of hermit life in Paris had been but poor preparation for real life in Chicago.

It was some time later when the first customer came – a painter whom he had known slightly in Paris. He had an order for a portrait of a dead boy, and wanted a mask taken before the youth was buried. The sculptor gathered together his materials and went. When he saw the face of the dead, the caricature of life it presented gave the young artist a sickening sensation. He got through with his work, but he did not sleep that night. He never heard of the success of the portrait, and no one ever spoke of paying him for the mask. Some weeks later there came a call for a death mask of a fine old gentleman, with a prospect of a marble bust if prices were low enough. This time the plaster hardened a little too rapidly, and the nervous sculptor had to hurry in cutting the mold with a string. When he finished his task he was soaking with perspiration, and he went home as limp as a rag. He had the precious mold under his arm, however, and got the order for the bust. With the assistance of a tintype and the contradictory criticisms of friends and relatives of the deceased he managed to make a portrait which was unveiled with much enthusiasm in public and justly criticized in private. And the evening and the morning were the first bust.

From that time on the business flourished. No one has wanted anything of the sculptor that he wished to do. No one thinks of posing for him alive, but after long illness, when at last the spark has flown and the poor, unfurnished tenement lies useless and without expression, the eyes closed, the cheeks sunken – then they want him to come and gather his data to make a living man again!

So the sculptor has made casts of dead folk of all stations, of sweet-faced women, of grand old men, and of new babies with funny, infantile features in low relief upon their little heads. He has visited humble homes and the wealthiest of our city. He has gone to receiving vaults in bitter-cold weather and nearly frozen to death among the still sleepers. He has made casts of diphtheria "cases," and learned of it afterward. He has visited death chambers at midnight. He has cast from masses of human clay dead a month, and he has waited for the last gasp. And he frankly acknowledges that he does not enjoy it. This is not the kind of "art" that he bargained for. It is not the profession which he thought he had chosen.

Dr. Duchenne de Boulogne demonstrated, long ago, that a paralyzed face was interesting when the muscles were played upon by a galvante battery. Occasionally one meets with a countenance which seems to require this treatment in order to put expression into it, but, generally speaking, every living face is of interest to the artist. There is always construction and modeling, and every trace of tension means something. It is surprising how much shows through. People model their own faces largely, and press and pinch and chisel them into shape. Some are experts and make good jobs of it. Many a homely visage grows bright and winning and even handsome as the years roll by. But, alas! There are many of these unconscious, unwilling sculptors who are making fearful botches of the one piece of work required of them. They put a lifetime upon it, and at the end it is only fit for the claybox where we are all dumped sooner or later. Nature seems to start us out a little unfairly. Some are well shaped before they begin. Some are beautiful outwardly and some have serene, noble faces, but there is always work to be done upon them. These gifts of person are fortunate inheritances, but they must be "made good" and made to take on significance by the possessor.

The bumps on some foreheads look vastly impressive, but they really stand for nothing at all. Not so with the activity of the face. The different ways in which eyelids close may mark a bad man or a pure man. A slight accent at the wing of the nose tells a volume. Phrenology may be out of date and palmistry may be only an ingenious diversion, but the face has a language which all men, the world over, both read and write. We may make mistakes, but we trust our interpretation of a face in preference to a hundred testimonials of character.

An artist is happy in studying the wonderful mechanisms of the human countenance, in discovering the slight differences, the variations from a standard type, which make the individual. He delights in reading the autographic inscription of him who dwells within. He catches glimpses of the soul peering through the eyes or lurking behind closed shutters. The topography of a face is fascinating only because it means something. What his is the artist reads according to his grasp and power of divination. He puts it into his work for others to read according to his skill and his sympathy with his subject. He ought to be more than a camera, and he should be able to see and know his subject at his best.

In addition to working on commission, Taft frequently created portraits just because he was interested in the individuals he was sculpting, and many of these remained in plaster.[69] Author Robert Moulton explained: "While he has reached that place where he might have commissions for all he could do, it is interesting to note that he frequently plans and executes a work without the slightest suggestion of an order, simply because the idea dominates him and demands to be put in some imperishable form."[70] Taft researcher Timothy Garvey wrote an interesting article in which he selected eight busts Taft had sculpted of friends and detailed how Taft's affection for these characters helped to create especially sensitive and loving likenesses.[71]

Plaster, bronze, and marble busts, too numerous to mention, sit in the Chicago Public Library, at the Krannert Art Museum in Urbana, the University of Chicago, the Chicago History Museum, Northwestern University, Beloit College, the University of Illinois, and the Oregon Public Library, among other places.

Busts (clockwise from top left): Ella Pomeroy Belden (1895-96, Lorado Taft Museum, Elmwood, Ill.)
Prof. George Washington Northrup (1898, Swift Hall, University of Chicago)
Pres. Edward Dwight Eaton (1912, Eaton Chapel, Beloit College, Beloit, Wis.)
Mrs. Wallace Heckman (1905-10, Eagle's Nest Art Colony Collection, Oregon, Ill.)
Ozora Stearns Davis (front, 1932) and Franklin Woodbury Fisk (1896, Chicago Theological Seminary)
Pres. George F. Magoun (1890, Goodnow Hall, Grinnell College, Grinnell, Iowa)
Silas B. Cobb (1894, Cobb Hall, University of Chicago)
(center) John Crerar (1891, Crerar Library, University of Chicago)

Frances Willard

Taft's plaster medallion of Frances Willard on display at the Rest Cottage

Frances Willard, noted temperance leader, suffragist, and founder of the Woman's Christian Temperance Union (WCTU) was one of Taft's more loyal fans. She lived in Evanston, Ill., just a few blocks from the house where Lorado and Carrie lived, and she was so impressed with Taft's work that she included his picture and biography in her book, *A Classic Town: The Story of Evanston by "An Old Timer."*[72] She commissioned Taft to sculpt plaster medallions of herself and her mother that are now on display at her Evanston home, Rest Cottage.[73]

Willard encouraged Susan B. Anthony, well-known women's rights leader, to commission Taft to design a bust for display at the World's Columbian Exposition in 1893. Anthony at first agreed to sit for Taft, but later yielded to those feminists who said that the bust should be sculpted by a woman. Willard wrote her: "Please do not take counsel of women who are so prejudiced that, as I once heard said, they would not allow a male grasshopper to chirp on their lawn; but out of your own great heart, refuse to set an example to such folly." Anthony relented, and Taft completed the bust, but Anthony was not pleased with it and it was destroyed after the fair.[74]

Taft creating Willard's bust for Northwestern University

(Inset) The marble bust (1898) in the University Archives

In 1898 John C. Shaffer planned to present a marble bust of Willard to Northwestern University. In preparation he gave Willard "full freedom to select any of the world's best sculptors."[75] Willard's friend Lady Henry Somerset proposed a number of prominent European artists, but Willard insisted on commissioning Taft, and sittings began only two months before she died. "It lacks only the power of speech," said Frank P. Crandon at the dedication.[76]

Taft later was commissioned to craft a similar bust in bronze for the Hall of Fame for Great Americans at New York University (now Bronx Community College); it was unveiled in 1923.[77] And in 1931, the WCTU commissioned Taft to create another bronze bust for display in the Willard Memorial Library located behind the Rest Cottage.

In 1929, the WCTU asked Taft to design a low relief panel of Willard that was unveiled in the Indiana state capitol rotunda to commemorate the 50th anniversary of the election of Willard to the presidency of the WCTU. Taft charged only for the bronze casting and provided his design for no charge. Governor Leslie accepted the plaque for the commonwealth of Indiana, and a grand celebration was held:

> *"Following the program a Youth Parade was held, testifying to the interest of young people in the great movement for sobriety, law observance, and law enforcement. Included were 4,750 children and youth from Sunday schools, Boy Scouts, Girl Scouts, Camp Fire Girls, and Salvation Army who marched through the capitol laying flowers at the base of the plaque in tribute to Willard. At the same time planes flying overhead dropped flowers. ... Included with the flowers was a large number of temperance leaflets which were eagerly caught and carried away...."[78]*

It is interesting that Taft's depictions of Willard never included her glasses, without which she was never seen in public. Shaffer wanted the rims of her glasses to be imitated in the marble bust he gave to Northwestern University, "but the task is one that sculptors have yet to master successfully and was not attempted," the *Chicago Times-Herald* reported.[79] (Taft had sculpted a bust of Horace Spencer Fiske in 1895, complete with glasses, so it could be done.) The marble bust, which has until recently been on display at the Northwestern University library, was moved to the University Archives after it was cleaned ... because students kept insisting on using pencil to draw glasses on her.

From top, the Hall of Fame for Great Americans; the plaque mounted in the rotunda of the Indiana State Capitol building (1929); and Willard's bust at the WCTU Willard Memorial Library (1931) which was a copy of the bust created for the Hall of Fame in 1923

War Memorials

$\mathcal{C}$reating Civil War monuments proved to be a ready source of work for Taft as he developed his reputation as a sculptor, although he had other projects he would rather have been doing. "He also told us, laughingly, that he made a few soldiers' monuments, and was quite thankful afterwards that he did not sign them," wrote Trygve Rovelstad.[80]

(Clockwise, from left)
Soldier's Monument in Oregon, Ill. (1916);
War Monument in Mt. Carroll, Ill. (1891);
and War Memorial in Winchester, Ind. (1892),
with inset of frieze also designed by Taft

The battlefield at Gettysburg needed memorials for its new park, and Taft was commissioned to create four different pieces: three battle scenes in relief and a low relief panel on the monument to George Custer.[81] At the National Military Park in Vicksburg, Miss., his statue of Admiral David Dixon Porter (1911) joins three other statues at the base of a huge obelisk dedicated to the U.S. Navy.

(Clockwise, from left) Custer's Monument at Gettysburg (1889);
Admiral Porter at Vicksburg (1911);
monuments at Gettysburg (1889) for 5th Michigan Infantry;
4th Michigan Infantry; and 3rd Michigan Infantry

Taft's war monument work extended past the first World War: He was commissioned to design the "Victory" monument (1922) at Victory Park in Danville, Ill., honoring "those who participated in the World's War of 1914 and 1918."

Models were made for war memorials in Omaha, Neb., and Albany, N.Y., both involving large figure groupings, but neither was completed.

He also created a dramatic and moving grouping of soldiers called "Defense of the Flag." There are three different versions of this piece: one for the battlefield at Chickamauga, Ga. (1894); one for Jackson, Mich. (1904); and one for the national cemetery in Marion, Ind. (1915)[82]. Jackson claims theirs is the best version:

> *"Several features distinguish the Jackson cast from the other two sculptures of the same title. In Jackson, the middle and wounded figures wear longer coats. The head of the kneeling figure is different than its cousins in Tennessee and Indiana, and here his backpack is between his legs rather than on his back. The standard bearer's right arm is not positioned like those on the out-of-state sculptures, and the flag on the Michigan monument is much fuller. It forms a frame or backdrop for the sculptural group rather than a finial as it does on the other two casts of Defense of the Flag. These changes from the original design at Chickamauga and its replica at Marion mark Jackson's sculpture as the more mature work. They simplify the composition and strengthen it."[83]*

(Above) "Victory" monument in Danville, Ill. (1922)

(Below) Models for war memorials in Albany, N.Y., and Omaha, Neb. (not completed)

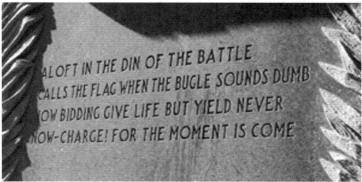

ALOFT IN THE DIN OF THE BATTLE
CALLS THE FLAG WHEN THE BUGLE SOUNDS DUMB
NOW BIDDING GIVE LIFE BUT YIELD NEVER
NOW-CHARGE! FOR THE MOMENT IS COME

(Clockwise, from lower left)
Incised quote, Jackson monument;
Jackson monument close up;
Marion, Ind. (1915), monument;
Jackson, Mich., monument (1904);
and Chickamauga, Ga., monument (1894)

Grave Memorials

New American sculptors also found work creating grave memorials, and Taft was no exception. "Eternal Silence" (1909) has become one of the most often visited tombs in Chicago's Graceland Cemetery. This heavily draped bronze figure, face mysteriously shrouded, eight feet tall and reflected in its polished granite backdrop, honors Dexter Graves, who had brought 13 families from Ohio in 1831 to settle in Chicago. This theme of a figure that is hooded or has a heavily shadowed face seemed to fascinate Taft and several other sculptors of the period, wrote Williams. He pointed out that Taft produced at least a dozen variations of this device.[84] Much of the intrigue of this cloaked figure in Graceland Cemetery comes from the fact that the cloak has oxidized to a bright green while his face has turned black.

"Eternal Silence" (1909)

(Above, left) "Recording Angel "(1923)
(Above, right) Foote Memorial (1923)

Taft also created several bronze memorials depicting powerful and beautiful women. The bronze "Recording Angel" (1923) was commissioned by Clarence Shaler in honor of his wife; it sits in Forest Mound Cemetery in Waupun, Wisc. and was listed on the National Register of Historic Places in 1974.[85] That same year, Taft was commissioned to create the William A. Foote Memorial (1923) that sits in Woodland Cemetery in Jackson, Mich. If the figure on the memorial should stand, she would be roughly twice lifesize.[86]

Many years later, Taft created another memorial in Graceland Cemetery, this time in indestructible black granite: "The Crusader" (1931) is a 10-foot-tall, impressive figure of a knight in medieval armor to memorialize Victor Lawson, publisher of the *Chicago Daily News* from 1876 to 1925.

"The Crusader" (1931)

Columbian Exposition

y the age of 33 — 1893 — Taft was without a doubt the outstanding artist in his field in Chicago, and he was invited to take responsibility for the art at the 1893 World's Columbian Exposition. Daniel Chester French and Frederick MacMonnies produced the two largest and most spectacular sculptural projects for the fair,[87] but William LeBaron Jenney, who was architect of the Horticulture Building, chose Taft to decorate his building. It was said at the time that Jenney gave Taft more freedom in the sculptural design than was allowed other sculptors on the other exposition buildings.[88]

(Clockwise, from lower left) "The Awakening of the Flowers" and "The Sleep of the Flowers." "Pomona" and "Flora" were positioned in the vestibule to the left and right of the entrance.

His sculpted figure groups, "The Sleep of the Flowers" and "The Awakening of the Flowers," each approximately eight feet tall, stood on either side of the entrance. Large statues of "Flora" and "Pomona" stood in the vestibule, and a frieze of cupids bearing garlands topped the composition. These were Taft's first designs on a heroic scale and the National Commission for the exposition awarded him a Designers' Medal for this work.[89] (The entire fair was made to be temporary, however. Taft's work that wasn't immediately demolished was soon destroyed in an 1894 fire.)[90]

Taft later compared his working at the Fair to that of working on the Parthenon in Athens after the second Persian War, or Florence during the Renaissance.[91] He felt challenged and creative, and he thrived among the many talented artists and architects who were working to create the "Great White City."

Other sculptors who had created statues and groups for the fair had sent models one-quarter the final size for enlargement in plaster. When Taft finished his work on the Horticulture Building, he was asked to take charge of enlarging these pieces for display in various exhibition buildings. Daniel Burnham, the fair's chief of construction, authorized him to hire as many people as he could find to do the work. It was not an accepted practice to hire women as sculptors at that time, but, Taft wrote, "When I told Mr. Burnham that I had several young women whom I would like to employ, he said that was all right, to employ anyone who could do the work – white rabbits if they would help out."

Taft's sister, Zulime, was one of these women; she wrote that they were paid $5 a day and $7.50 for overtime. This group of talented women sculptors who kept the name "the White Rabbits" throughout their lives included Zulime (Garland), Julia Bracken (Wendt), Carrie Brooks (MacNeil), Bessie Potter (Vonnoh), Janet Scudder, and Enid Yandell.[92] Taft also arranged for some of these assistants to get additional work, especially on the Women's Building and for several state buildings.[93]

Janet Scudder included a description of the hectic scene inside the Horticulture Building in an autobiography:

> "It was like some giant's studio; and surely crowded with giants as we filled it with those huge figures, which when finished, were hauled away and put into position on the buildings. In the winter we were kept from freezing by large braziers filled with glowing fires; in the summer we were saved from heat prostration by awnings that were stretched across the roof and sprayed with water ... to see the white rabbits at work was one of the sights of those days."[94]

Taft's studio in the Horticulture Building as it appeared August 24, 1892.
Taft is in the foreground conferring with Julia Bracken, who worked on the "Sleep of the Flowers."
Busy in the background are other members of his studio group.

Taft later sculpted two figure groupings in Italian marble for the Fernery at Chicago's Garfield Park Conservatory: "Idyll" and "Pastoral" (1913). He affectionately called them his "Little Fool Groups."[95]

(Above) "Idyll" sits to the left of the entrance to the Fernery, and "Pastoral" sits to the right. At the base of "Pastoral" sit two little white rabbits (inset) – no doubt a reference to the hard-working women of the Columbian Exposition.

(Left) A vintage postcard shows the sculptures' original positioning inside the Fernery.

Fountains

Taft's sculptural repertoire also included a variety of fountains. One of his first commissions after arriving in Chicago — so fresh from Paris — was to model a statue of the Marquis de Lafayette for the top of a fountain in Lafayette, Ind., in 1886. This design was actually just a copy of a well-known statue that Bartholdi had crafted for New York City ten years earlier.[96]

Taft's "Ferguson Fountain of the Great Lakes," dedicated on September 9, 1913, was the first commission of the newly established B.F. Ferguson Monument Fund — a million-dollar bequest of Chicago merchant Benjamin F. Ferguson specifically to finance art that would beautify the city — and it was Taft's first major assignment after his work on the Columbian Exposition.

Taft's work had garnered much attention at the fair, but art collectors in Chicago still preferred the established work of foreign masters. "Whether drawn to old masters or more contemporary artists, wealthy Chicagoans like Bertha Honore Palmer, Sara Hallowell, Martin A. Ryerson, and Charles T. Yerkes virtually always favored the works of Europeans and eastern artists when amassing their personal collections," one author explained.[97] Timothy J. Garvey, who researched in great detail Taft's rocky relationship with Chicago's Ferguson Fund in *Public Sculptor: Lorado Taft and the Beautification of Chicago*,[98] elaborated:

> *"Few of the other sculptors and painters who participated in the creation of the White City found sufficient local interest outside Jackson Park to warrant extending their time in Chicago long beyond the end of the fair. From the major figures like Saint-Gaudens and French to young hopefuls like Janet Scudder, Lee Lawrie, and Andrew O'Connor, most simply finished their work and departed for more supportive environs."[99]*

Taft told the audience at the fountain's dedication ceremonies about the "long and dreary period after the World's Fair, a hopeless eternity of depression and longing" during which opportunities were few and slight. This commission, he said, was a turning point in his career.[100] "It came over me gradually," he recalled, "that the coy attitude of our artists, like a girl waiting to be proposed to, was not a success. That while our public needed sculpture, it did not know it and never would guess it unless someone showed it what it wanted!"[101]

Even as the creation of the Ferguson Fund was being discussed, Taft knew this philanthropy could be his stepping stone to creating major sculptures. He immediately began designing this fountain and planned to place it in Grant Park. It would personify the five lakes as splendid classical female figures, each holding a conch shell, posed in such a way that the running streams of water would flow from one shell to another.

At the dedication ceremonies, Taft explained how his idea for the fountain came to be:

> *"It happened in this way: Almost 20 years ago – I remember it was soon after the World's Fair – I was on my way, one evening, to Evanston, and chanced to sit beside Mr. [Daniel] Burnham. We were talking of the triumphs of that most beautiful of all expositions, and Mr. Burnham criticized gently the lack of initiative of our sculptors, remarking that he was sorry that none of us had thought to make a fountain personifying the Great Lakes. I recognized at once the beauty of the suggestion and felt appropriately ashamed that none of us should have thought of it. Later I made the sketch which has developed in the course of years into the group before you. … The motif of the group is not profound. I have sometimes wondered if it were not too obvious. "Lake Superior" on high and "Lake Michigan" at the side both empty into the basin of "Lake Huron," who sends the waters on to "Lake Erie" whence "Lake Ontario" receives them. As they escape from her basin and hasten into the unknown, she reaches wistfully after them as though questioning whether she has been neglectful of her charge…"[102]*

One of Taft's first commissions was a statue of Lafayette for a fountain next to the county courthouse in Lafayette, Ind. (1886)

Taft had finished a plaster version of the fountain by mid-January of 1906.[103] That model was placed on view at the Art Institute's annual exhibition of works by Chicago local artists, and it took the Chicago Municipal Art League's prize for the best work of sculpture.[104] One writer recommending various recipients for the Fund's first commission suggested that Chicago "already has at least one man, Lorado Taft, who is a national figure in that art."[105]

In 1907, as expected, Taft's "Fountain of the Great Lakes" was chosen as the first recipient of the fund. The contract provided a sum of $38,000 to cover the costs of creation, fabrication, and installation of the work, with payments scheduled for specific points over the three years allotted for completion of the project.[106]

However, it actually took six more years for the piece to be dedicated. (A. Montgomery Ward was opposed to the introduction of new buildings in Grant Park and had initiated legal proceedings. The trustees of the Ferguson Fund, who had hoped Taft's fountain could have a prestigious site in the new downtown park, felt that placing the fountain in the park should be delayed until the matter was settled.)[107] As Taft waited and waited for the matter to be resolved, a Buffalo merchant tried to persuade him to place his work in Buffalo, but Taft decided to wait a bit longer.[108] In the spring of 1913 the model was finally sent to the foundry of Jules Berchem,[109] and the fountain did indeed end up in Grant Park, sited in front of the south wall of the Art Institute.

(Below) a photo of the "Ferguson Fountain of the Great Lakes" in its original position on the south side of the Art Institute

(Right) The plaque dedicated to Ferguson is attached to the back of the fountain, documented here by a most diligent photographer.

"Ferguson Fountain of the Great Lakes" (1913)

Weller pointed out that, in Burnham's well-publicized *1909 Plan for the City of Chicago*, "The only work of sculpture reproduced in [the] book is a small illustration of Taft's "Fountain of the Great Lakes," at that time only to be seen in a small preliminary sketch model."[110] Burnham apparently was pleased with the conversation he and Taft had had on that train to Evanston.

During the entire period from Taft's commission to the fountain's dedication, newspapers and periodicals gave the design considerable attention. Taft was interviewed repeatedly, and the message was that the piece would be a great success. "Like no other public sculpture in the city," Garvey wrote, "this fountain captured the attention and imagination of a public for whom it represented the qualities and ideals believed important in such works."[111]

But in *Public Sculptor* Garvey detailed a shift in sentiment, even as the fountain was being commissioned, when people began to voice their criticism for Taft's design. One of the chief complaints was that there was little connection between his dignified bronze classical figures and the rather tumultuous character of the Great Lakes themselves. Literary critic and poet Harriet Monroe, usually a fan of Taft's work, wrote that the sculptor's women were vaguely disappointing to her, reflecting neither the geographic configuration of the lakes nor the true spirit of the nation's inland seas."[112] Garvey wrote that, on the morning of the dedication, the *Chicago Daily News* published a photomontage, overlaying a photo of Taft's fountain with a photo of Lake Michigan, crashing violently against a battered breakwater and throwing spray to heights seemingly greater than the sculpture itself.[113]

There was an additional subject for criticism: The women in Taft's fountain were partially nude. Only three months before the fountain was set in place outside the Art Institute, Chicago's City Council had passed an ordinance banning any art representing a person in a nude state displayed in any place that could be seen from a public highway or in a public place frequented by children.[114] Taft's fountain was not removed, but the complaints continued.

The "Ferguson Fountain of the Great Lakes" was later moved to a landscaped park nestled in the south end of the extended museum complex. A low relief portrait of Ferguson in bronze between two bronze panels of laurel branches, attached to the back of the fountain's granite block plinth, is no longer accessible to the public.[115] "Now the maiden Erie, who originally faced east like her namesake, faces north-northwest, destroying the symbolism of Taft's composition," one columnist pointed out, and quoted another author: "The resiting showed not just indifference toward both artist and patron, but insult."[116]

From an undated newspaper article, a photo of Grinnell College co-eds portraying Taft's "Fountain of the Great Lakes" on the college campus. In the group are Margaret Napier and Beulah Conlee of Chicago, Josephine Orr of Lincoln, Neb., and Jewell Rutherford and Faith Somers of Grinnell, Iowa.

Taft's lighthearted Trotter Fountain (1911) in Withers Park in Bloomington, Ill., represents childhood, animal life, and pioneer life, with a bear cub on the south end and a dog on the north, and Native American children. A Native American maiden stands at each end with an urn on her shoulder, from which a stream of water runs into the basin below. Williams wrote: "Taft, with his pupils Janet Scudder and Bessie Potter Vonnoh, was an early explorer of fanciful park and garden sculpture, of groups without serious intent, of statues 'for the fun of it.'"[117] Taft designed this memorial to the Trotter family, but assistants from his Chicago studio did the actual sculpting of the Georgia marble. After the dedication ceremonies, Swiss-born Walter Zimmerman spent about two months in Bloomington finishing up the fountain. "He does not speak the English language very fluently," *The Pantagraph* reported, "but is a very intelligent and entertaining man to talk to."[118]

Trotter Fountain (1911), designed "without serious intent"

Soon after, in 1912, entries were sought for a new "Columbus Fountain" to sit in front of Union Station in Washington, D.C. The selection commission adopted a fountain design by Daniel Burnham, who had designed the station itself, and selected Taft to provide the sculptural features.[119] Here, in a more "down-to-earth" theme than the classical figures of the "Fountain of the Great Lakes," a figurehead called "Discovery" stands at the prow of a ship, with Christopher Columbus standing behind it, with a globe supported by four American eagles high above him on a 45-foot-tall shaft, and with figures of a New World Native American and an elderly Old World European man and haughty lions seated at either end.

> *"It will sit on the plaza in front of the Union Station…. No more fortunate or appropriate site for the memorial could possibly have been selected. Situated at the gateway of the nation's capital, it will be the first and the last thing to greet the eyes of the millions of visitors who annually journey there. And it seems altogether fitting that this monument to the discoverer of a new world should stand in the capital of its greatest country."[120]*

Although this fountain has been essentially well maintained, on October 12, 1992, on the 500th anniversary of Columbus's reaching land, Native Americans poured blood over the monument in protest, calling the fountain "another symbol of white supremacy."[121]

(Above) The concept of Columbus Fountain (1912) was designed by Daniel Burnham, and the sculptural features were completed by Taft. The figurehead curving outward from the figure of Columbus is called "Discovery."

(Facing page) Thatcher Fountain in Denver, Colo. (1918). Figure groupings surround the magnificent female figure of Colorado. They are called "Learning," "Loyalty," and "Love."

THE GIFT OF
JOSEPH ADDISON THATCHER
TO THE
CITY OF DENVER
1918

Lynn Allyn Young   37

Around 1918, Joseph Addison Thatcher, a very successful banker in Colorado's early history, paid Taft $100,000 to design a fountain as a gift to the city of Denver.[122] Thatcher Fountain in Denver's City Park depicts Colorado as a powerful woman standing 18 feet tall on a central pedestal and holding a sword and shield, with groups of figures circling the main figure named "Loyalty," "Learning," and "Love."

Taft's "Fish Boys" Fountain (1920s) is located in Mix Park in Oregon, Ill. Two cherubic figures, each five feet tall, kneel on the sides of a shallow pool and hold dolphins that spout water. The original figures were designed and cast in bronze as part of the "Fountain of the Great Lakes." These in Mix Park are constructed of the special composite of concrete and crushed quartz also used to cover the "Fountain of Time."

(Above) The "Fish Boys" in the fountain in Oregon, Ill., (1920s) are replicas of the cherubs on either side of the Ferguson Fountain of the Great Lakes.

(Inset) Taft working on one of the fish boy statues

Abraham Lincoln, Stephen Douglas, and other historical figures

braham Lincoln and Stephen Douglas were of special interest to Taft. He created a low-relief panel depicting Douglas (1901) in Mandel Hall at the University of Chicago, and a second monument to Douglas (1913) in Douglas's birthplace of Brandon, Vt., using the same design. (It is possible that his interest in Douglas began because his wife, Ada, was originally from Brandon.)

The plaque of Douglas at the University of Chicago (1901) (left) and an identical plaque on a monument in Brandon, Vt. (1913)

His statue of "Lincoln, the Young Lawyer" (1927) – depicting him as a young lawyer trying cases at the Champaign County Courthouse -- stands in Carle Park in Urbana, Ill., and was added to the National Register of Historic Places in 2004. Because Lincoln visited Urbana on the circuit, this bronze masterpiece originally stood at the Urbana-Lincoln Hotel, a block from the courthouse where he practiced law. Soon after its dedication, however, it was moved to the park across the street from the high school, at which time Taft asked that it be rotated from east to southeast so "the sun could always shine down upon his face." The statue was a gift from Judge and Mrs. J.O. Cunningham, who had been personal friends of Lincoln after they befriended him during his travels on the Eighth Judicial Circuit.[123] Siegfried Weng, who studied with and became lecture assistant to Taft before moving on to a successful arts career, posed for the Lincoln sculpture, being exactly Lincoln's height: 6 feet, 4 inches.[124]

Williams wrote, "With the plethora of sculptured Great Emancipators in the land, Taft deserves credit for creating an original, sensible, and dignified statue."[125] He included a quote from Taft that explained how he thought long and hard about how to represent Lincoln:

> *"I have so long adored Saint-Gaudens' 'Lincoln' which has stood at the entrance of our Chicago Lincoln Park since 1887, that it had become to my mind practically the final word. It seemed impossible to think of Lincoln in any other guise or attitude. When, therefore, I was asked to make a Lincoln statue for my almost-home-town of Urbana, Illinois, I found myself vastly troubled. Presently out of the mists came a gleam of hope: Lincoln was a companionable young man when he was wont to visit Urbana as a lawyer. I need not show him as a man of sorrows, but as an earnest, good humored orator stating his case. I shall model him leaning slightly backward, supported by both hands on a desk."[126]*

A smaller version of Taft's Lincoln statue stands on the ground floor gallery of Lincoln's Tomb in Springfield, Ill., among other Lincoln depictions by Daniel Chester French, Fred M. Torrey, Leonard Crunelle, Adolph Weinman, and Augustus St. Gaudens. In 1927 Taft gave a matching five-foot bronzed plaster statue of Lincoln to the John H. Vanderpoel Art Association in the Chicago suburb of Beverly, and he also authorized the

*(Clockwise, from lower left) Taft working on the "Young Lincoln" statue;
the smaller statue of Lincoln on display in Lincoln's tomb (dedicated July 3, 1927);
and the statue (1927) "facing the sun" in Urbana's Carle Park*

production of more than ten five-foot-tall plaster copies to be presented to high schools, several of which are still in existence.

Taft designed many other historical figures, either as commissions or as contest entries. Schuyler Colfax (1887), standing in Indianapolis's University Park, was one of his first commissions and was the first statue in the park. (Colfax was vice president to Grant and first vice president to come from Indiana.) Some critics said this was not one of Taft's best works, describing it as wooden, unnatural, with "a stride about to propel the poor man off his perch atop the squat shaft of the pedestal."[127] Taft was pleased to have obtained the job, but later he related his embarrassment at having designed such "effigies" and his "satisfaction that he had not captured all the commissions he sought."[128]

(Above) Schuyler Colfax (1887), and the panel mounted on the statue's base that depicts the Bible story of Rebecca giving water to Abraham's man at the well

(Inset) Taft designed the low-relief panel on the back of the Grant statue after an scene by Thure de Thulstrup, a well-known illustrator of military scenes. Taft used horse images only twice, and this image closely resembles Thulstrup's renderings.

Ulysses S. Grant (1889) in the middle of historic Fort Leavenworth

Taft's statue of Ulysses S. Grant (1889) stands prominently at the intersection of Grant and Kearney avenues on the grounds of historic Fort Leavenworth, Kan. Nearly $5,000 for the commission was raised from the soldiers and civilians on the post, and from leading citizens of Kansas and Missouri.[129] This was the first statue of its kind to be erected in the West to an officer of the United States Army, and the idea for its commission was made within a week after Grant's death. "An audience of 10,000 people, including public men, Federal and Confederate, from all parts of the country," was present for the unveiling.[130]

And a monumental statue of George Washington (1909) is centrally positioned on the campus of the University of Washington in Seattle, unveiled in time for the opening of the Alaska Yukon Pacific Exposition. Four-year-old Eleanor Washington Caldwell, George Washington's great grandniece, unveiled the statue on Flag Day.[131] In her book, Ada Taft remembers Taft working on the 15-foot statue on the terrace in back of their studio at the Eagle's Nest Colony; their youngest daughter sat on a stool next to her father and called the first president "Georgie Wash."[132]

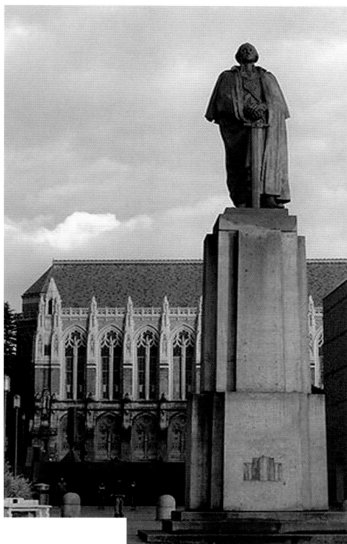

(Clockwise, from right) Taft's statue of Washington (1909) gazes down Campus Parkway with Suzzallo Library in the background.

Vintage photos show the statue being hoisted onto a temporary base and crowds gathering for the dedication ceremony.

A much simpler monument honors a woman who made history in the small town of White Hall, Ill.: Annie Louise Keller saved 16 children but sacrificed her own life when a tornado demolished the Centerville School building on April 19, 1927. The pink Tennessee marble sculpture shows Keller shielding a young boy and girl; it was paid for with pennies donated by Illinois school children, and on the side are inscribed the names of the 21 pupils who were enrolled in the school at that time. Mary Keller, sister of Annie Louise, modeled for Taft "so that the symbolism and inspired grouping of the figures might have the added value of representing the features of Annie Louise Keller."[133] The monument was completed in 1929; it sits on the edge of White Hall's Whiteside Park.

Annie Louise Keller (1929)

Low-relief panels

ow-relief bronze panels (sometimes referred to as "stiacciato") were popular ways to memorialize people and historical events at the time, and Taft received many commissions for them. Williams suggested in his dissertation that Taft was best at low-relief, and often his other works can be seen as panels that were developed into more three-dimensional pieces.[134]

A young Bobs Roberts (1931) in Comer Children's Hospital

Taft's portrait of "Bobs" (1931) is a charming image of Bobs Roberts, who died as a child. The Bobs Roberts Memorial Hospital for Children treated patients for the University of Chicago Department of Pediatrics until the opening of Wyler Children's Hospital in 1967. The piece is now owned by Comer Children's Hospital, which replaced Wyler.

And a relief portrait of Katharine Lucinda Sharp (1921), head librarian and director of the University of Illinois Library School beginning in 1899, is elegantly displayed in the great hall of the university's main library.

Other bronze portraits are scattered around the United States: Charles Allen Marsh (1921), tucked in a dark northeast corner of Hyde Park Union Church in Chicago and eclipsed by the glow of the sanctuary's impressive Tiffany stained glass windows; O. Henry (1914), in the reference area of the State Library in Raleigh, N.C.; Henry Harkness Stoek (1925), at the School of Engineering at the University of Illinois; Stephen Moulton Babcock (1934), in the Biochemistry Building of the University of Wisconsin at Madison; Jonathan Prentiss Dolliver (1925), at Dolliver Memorial State Park in Iowa; Melville A. Scovell (1914), at the Kentucky State Agricultural Experiment Station in Lexington, Ky.; and George Westinghouse (1915), originally at the East Pittsburgh Works of the Westinghouse Electric Corporation, Pittsburgh, Pa., and now in storage at Pittsburgh's Heinz History Center.[135]

Katharine Lucinda Sharp (1921)

Taft's large, low-relief depiction of the tragic fire at Chicago's Iroquois Theater (1910) is now mounted high on the north wall inside the west entrance to Chicago's City Hall, where hundreds of people walk by it daily but rarely stop to examine it. This tablet, in memory of the 600-plus adults and children who perished in a ghastly 1903 fire, was originally located at Chicago's Iroquois Memorial Hospital in the main reception room, but the building was demolished around 1951, and a janitor found it in the basement of City Hall in the 1960s. Mark Skertic wrote an article about this panel back in 1998 for the *Chicago Tribune* and quoted Michael Lash, then the city's director of public art. "No one knew what it was. No one knew how it got there. If it wasn't bronze and wasn't 200 pounds, it might've walked."[136] During its time in the City Hall entrance, it has had no identifying marker, but the plaque was rededicated in November, 2010, to celebrate its 100th year, and Taft has now been given the proper credit. "This is an interesting tale about an historic piece of art that becomes lost ..., then is rescued only to spend decades forgotten all over again -- while in plain view," said Alderman Edward Burke in his press release.[137]

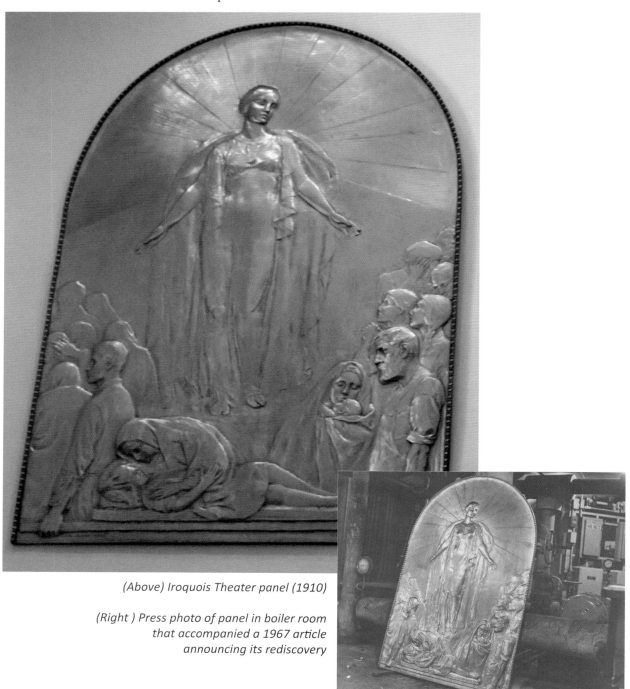

(Above) Iroquois Theater panel (1910)

(Right) Press photo of panel in boiler room that accompanied a 1967 article announcing its rediscovery

*The plaque to Jonathan Prentiss Dolliver is mounted directly to a boulder
in the middle of a state park that Dolliver helped to establish (1925).*

Medals

In 1916, the poet James Whitcomb Riley was to turn 65, and his friends decided to throw the party to end all parties. They wanted to devise a permanent souvenir to give to the 500 attendees. After deciding on a bronze medal, the planners contacted Taft to design it, despite the fact that he had never designed a medal before. Taft was deeply interested and enthusiastic — having known Riley personally — and came up with an intriguing design: On one side, a portrait of Riley in his prime, from a photo some 15 years earlier.[138] It says, "James Whitcomb Riley – Poet of Hope and Cheer – Lover and Friend of Mankind." On the other side, an idea taken from one of Riley's poems: the figure of Pan, playing his flute for a farmer and a small boy.[139] Several medals are on display in museums and have occasionally appeared on online auctions. The medal shown at right can be viewed at the Lilly Library at Indiana University.

A second medal design was never made permanent. In 1930, the Medallic Art Society began commissioning and distributing a series of medals twice a year. Almost all of the more conservative American sculptors eventually were asked to create a medal for this purpose, and it was Taft's turn in 1935. Taft's daughter, Emily, wrote an extensive description and provided illustrations of his design.[140] The whole medal is inscribed "Christianity in the Twentieth Century of our Lord." On one side, the central, monumental figure has a death's head and is decorated with a large cross on its chest. The two young men each hold pistols against each other's heads, while two aged men behind them urge them on. Above this group, the inscription reads: "On Earth Peace Good Will Toward Men." On the reverse side, the back of a hooded figure (resembling the Time figure on the "Fountain of Time" or the figure in the "Eternal Silence" memorial) gazes over the unending rows of graves marked with crosses. Taft told a reporter that his depiction of the young men with pistols was inspired by a visit to a French prison camp during World War I, where he observed just such boys and talked with them over their experiences and their reasons for fighting.[141]

Needless to say, this medal presented problems for the Society of Medalists, and they requested that Taft submit an alternate design. "It is a difficult subject for a medal…," they wrote, "the idea not beautiful or pleasant." Taft acknowledged this with, "I was sure the medal would be refused. [War is] organized murder – and we call ourselves Christian nations. Why should one not feel it a subject for satire?"[142] He proceeded to produce in reduced scale the "Fountain of the Great Lakes" on one side, with an idealized head of one of the figures on the reverse. Hundreds of this version were created, in a variety of sizes, and many are owned by museums around the country. Various sizes often show up on online auctions.

Midway Studios

Taft worked in a number of studios in Chicago, first in the Lydian Gallery at 103 South State Street, where he started a modeling class for young ladies.[143] He moved to the Athenaeum Building on State Street in 1894.[144] Another space, in 1898, was on the tenth floor of the Fine Arts Building on Chicago's Michigan Avenue.[145] The doors of the studios were opened on Saturday afternoons to visitors, a few of whom stayed for buffet supper.[146] This was the artistic pulse of the city.

> *"It was the ladies who sustained the vogue for studio visits. Artists outdid each other in providing exotic settings and tempting refreshments for these bands of roving aesthetes to drop in on. The artists tolerated the interruptions and the expense in the hope of impressing clients, with mixed results; many of the ladies apparently used the studios as convenient refuges from the crowds in the Loop's busy shops."[147]*

Taft was aware that opening his studios was good for public relations, but he complained to his family that the visitors were increasingly distracting – they "come in to look around and then are off again," he wrote. He might be in the middle of casting and would have to stop to talk; sometimes the noise of the crowds would make him lose his train of thought completely.[148]

In 1906 the University of Chicago leased him a large brick building at 60th and Ellis streets, originally stables. By the time Taft and his assistants were done renovating and erecting other buildings (two frame barns were moved in to accompany the brick barn), the complex included two dormitories and 13

Taft's studio in the Fine Arts Building

studios.[149] Taft said the studios were built "like the chambered nautilus, cell after cell."[150]

"Most of the studios opened onto a large covered court with a fireplace and a fountain, a marble-cutting room and a stage for occasional plays. At one end was the original plaster cast of Lorado's bronze group, the "Fountain of the Great Lakes." There was a kitchen adjoining the court, where the noonday meal was prepared for 10 to 25 artists and their friends. Lorado called the table for the noon meal the "groaning board."[151]

In 1929, the university needed this land to build a new women's dormitory, and the barn was moved east one block to 6016 South Ingleside Avenue, the various additions were reconstructed, and both were attached to an existing brick house where Taft and his family lived. (An addition was built in 1964.)[152]

(Above) The "groaning board" in a photo from 1915 or 1916: People include Nellie V. Walker, Paul Fjelde, George Ganierre, Agnes Fromen, Fred Torrey, Kathleen Robinson Ingles, Henry B. Fuller, Clyde Chandler, John J. Prasuhn, Leonard Crunelle, Fred Ingles, and Amy Nordstran.

(Right) An unsigned invitation to a Taft birthday party (1930s)

This area was located on the south side of the campus across from a mile-long grassy strip called the "Midway Plaisance." The Midway had been designed for the Columbian Exposition by Frederic Law Olmsted to connect Washington and Jackson parks; during the fair, the land was used to house tented displays and amusements that included a giant Ferris wheel.

As Taft's workload increased and he began working on bigger and bigger pieces at Midway Studios, he needed help. At times he had as many as 30 young assistants, a number of whom lived in the dormitory-type rooms in the complex.[153] Many of these assistants went on to become well-known artists, including Leonard Crunelle, Frederick C. Hibbard, Charles J. Mulligan, Trygve Rovelstad, and Nellie Walker. The studio was said to house "the largest concentration of sculptors under one roof in the world."[154] "It seemed for all the world like the household of one of the great artistic craftsmen of the Italian Renaissance in the days of Benvenuto Cellini transplanted into 20th-century America," wrote one reporter.[155]

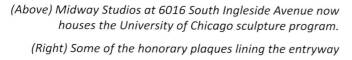

(Above) Midway Studios at 6016 South Ingleside Avenue now houses the University of Chicago sculpture program.

(Right) Some of the honorary plaques lining the entryway

> "To his students, Taft was referred to as 'Fra Lorado.' … [His] studio attracted many artists, intellectuals and writers, and his students and assistants were therefore exposed to some of the best minds and most influential cultural figures of the era. In addition to rigorous academic training, an immersion in technique and an understanding of the properties and potentials of materials, Taft stressed the higher moral and spiritual importance of art and the civic ideals associated with public art."[156]

On each April 29, Taft's birthday, the studio was redecorated for a program consisting of plays, dancing, and poetry.

> "Lorado's birthday was made a gala day. Each vied with the other in transforming the court into a Venetian palace or a desert scene with a black Bedouin tent. Sometimes there was a fancy dress ball, sometimes a grand banquet, when, donning their own or borrowed best clothes; they astonished each other by their good looks. Sometimes an original play was given, and real dramatic talent discovered."[157]

After Taft died in 1936, the studio's contents were given to the University of Illinois and the buildings fell into disrepair. But in the late 1950s, the University of Chicago began restoring the buildings to house its expanded fine-arts program. Midway Studios is now the home of the university's sculpture department. Although the interior is completely devoid of any evidence that Taft ever lived and worked there, plaques line its front door: It was named a National Historic Landmark in 1965, was listed on the National Register of Historic Places in 1966, and was made a Chicago Landmark in 1993. It is one of the four Chicago Registered Historic Places from the original October 15, 1966 National Register of Historic Places list (along with Chicago Pile-1 [the world's first artificial nuclear reactor], Hull House and Robie House).

The Gates of Paradise

Taft actually took one of his plays on the road: *The Gates of Paradise*. Written as a way to introduce school children to Renaissance sculpture, the script was completed in 1930 and produced the next year. For the set, he created a full-size model of "Andrea's Doors" that had been created for the Baptistry at Florence in the 1300s. In his dissertation, Williams described the plot:

> *The play begins in 1400, explaining that the residents of Florence have promised that, if they may be saved from a deadly plague, they will create a new set of bronze gates for the baptistry in thanks. Italian artists compete for the honor of constructing the gates and they study Andrea's doors as their model. Ghiberti wins the commission. The second act is in Donatello's studio 25 years later, complete with full-scale reproductions of Donatello's sculptures that were made at the Midway Studios. Ghiberti has completed his doors, and Florence is celebrating. (This act is to show students the life and work of 15th-century artists.) In the third act — another 25 years later — Ghiberti has completed a second set of doors that he likes better, and the city of Florence has come to him on his birthday to thank him for completing the project. Now Florence can once again become the artistic, cultural, and spiritual capital of the world!*

The first show, with an amateur cast, took place at Kelvyn Park High School in February of 1931; it was given again at the Goodman Theater in March and at Mandel Hall on the University of Chicago campus in April. All of these performances were paid for by Taft.[158]

A cast shot from The Gates of Paradise *showing Taft's immense full-size model of the original "Andrea's Doors" from the 1300s. Taft paid for all the performances.*

Dream Museum & Peep Shows

Throughout his life Taft accumulated a large collection of casts of great works of sculpture from all ages and countries, always hoping to organize them into a first-class museum. Ada wrote, "I shall have to acknowledge that my husband was just a little daft about museums."[159]

He set his hopes on housing them in the Columbian Exposition's Fine Arts Building (one of the few structures built to be permanent), and he prepared a proposal outlining a layout. He wrote:

> "Do you know that there is hardly a school-child in Chicago who has ever been privileged to see reproductions, even, of the masterpieces of ancient art? They never see the sculptures of the Parthenon, the Hermes of Praxiteles, the Victory of Samothrace, the Venus of Melos, the Augustus Caesar, the works of Donatello, the achievements of Michelangelo. ... I have been having the time of my life, planning a magnificent museum of architecture and sculpture, where the great works of the past may be studied and enjoyed. One essential feature is an unobstructed vista; a perspective of the continuity of civilization. The space required is a stretch, preferably east and west, of three city blocks, or a tract of say twelve hundred feet in length by perhaps four or five hundred feet in breadth."[160]

In 1926 the Chicago City Council authorized $5 million to restore the building as a convention auditorium with the east end as a museum.

Chicago retailer and philanthropist Julius Rosenwald also had his eyes on this building, proposing that the building be converted into an industrial museum, and he volunteered several million dollars to add to the city's appropriation. Chicago accepted Rosenwald's proposal, and Taft went back to the drawing board.

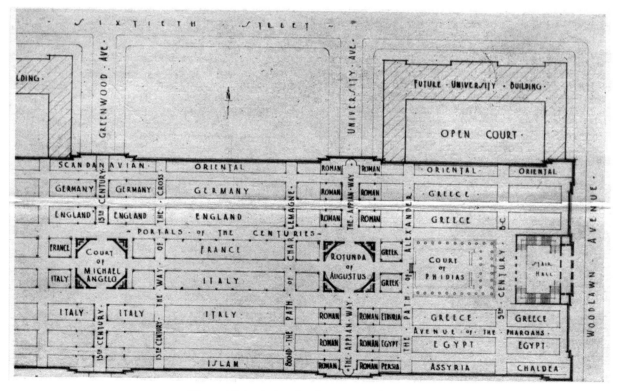

The published plan for the proposed museum

Los Angeles then offered Taft land on which to build a museum, at Griffith Park overlooking the city, but the project needed a financial benefactor, and benefactors were scarce during the Great Depression. By June 1934, Taft sought federal funding of the museum as part of a New Deal employment project, without success. In addition, his health began to fail, and the project was never completed. After his death, the project quickly lost its focus. In May 1938 the Los Angeles Art Association tried again to fulfill Taft's dream. They requested $950,000 from the Los Angeles County Board of Supervisors for a smaller but broader museum of music, sculpture, painting, dance and theater adjacent to the Otis Art Institute on Wilshire Boulevard. For a number of reasons, it wasn't built either.[161]

(Above) Taft planning the layout of his museum

(Left) The Fine Arts Building as it appeared at the time of the Columbian Exposition

Taft did, however, succeed in creating a smaller version of his museum: eight small dioramas that represented "a typical hour in the active life of a sculptor,"[162] each suggesting some dramatic event or period, and filled with not only small-scale figures of historical personages, but with reduced models of appropriate works of art. He called these his "peep shows." They ran all the way from Phidias and Praxiteles to Michelangelo and Claus Sluter.[163] The size varied but had a common scale of two inches equals one foot, and the average figure was 11 inches high.[164] The dioramas were made between 1927 and 1936 under the supervision of an assistant, Mary Webster, after Taft's plans.[165]

Several sets of these dioramas were created; one, previously owned by the University of Illinois World Heritage Museum, was sold at a state auction "because of lack of storage space"[166] and is now in anonymous private hands; and another is in storage at the Museum of Art in Evansville, Ind. However, another full set has been on full display at the Kenosha (Wisc.) Public Museum since 1938. These dioramas were installed in their present cases in 1953 and moved to a brand new building in 2001.

The Kenosha Public Museum houses a full set of Taft's Peep Shows. Each diorama comes with a detailed chart of who is depicted.

(Top right) studio of Phideas and (bottom) studio of Donatello

Eagle's Nest Colony

Taft's family — including his sister, Zulime, and her husband, novelist Hamlin Garland, and another sister, Turbia, who had married the painter Charles Francis Browne — spent summers in the late 1890s at Bass Lake, Ind., on property owned by relatives of sculptor Charles Mulligan, but the appearance of malaria in the vicinity forced them to leave in 1897.[167] Beginning in 1898, Taft, his family, his assistants, and an interesting assortment of artists, writers, and architects began spending their summers at a camp in Oregon, Ill.

Wallace Heckman, a Chicago attorney and patron of the arts (and eventually the business manager of the newly established University of Chicago), invited Taft to move the camp to his estate on the edge of the Rock River in Oregon. The art colonists entered into a lease that ran for as long as one of the founding members remained alive. Taft would arrive each year "accompanied by students and carrying hundreds of pounds of clay."[168] Each Labor Day, the group would "pay tribute" to the Heckmans for the use of the land. Led by Taft, as "chief," and with everyone dressed in costumes, each resident would solemnly pay his rent of "eighty-nine pennies, two slugs, and some postage."[169]

By 1904, the Eagle's Nest colony was so well established that Harriet Monroe wrote a feature for *House Beautiful* describing the picturesque summer community these enterprising artists had created.[170] Just as Taft had found the perfect circle of companions while working at the Columbian Exposition, here at the Eagle's Nest he and his colleagues could escape from modern society and focus on their art. The colony flourished until 1942, when Ralph Clarkson died.[171]

The Tafts' summer home, designed by Pond & Pond, is still used by Northern Illinois University.

A recent book by Jan Stilson, *Art and Beauty in the Heartland: The Story of the Eagle's Nest Camp at Oregon, Illinois, 1898-1942*,[172] tells the interesting story of the colony, and the Oregon Public Library houses a gallery of paintings and sculptures by Taft and other members of the group.[173] The buildings Taft and his friends constructed are still there, next to what is now Lowden State Park, and are used as part of the Lorado Taft Field Campus for Outdoor Education of Northern Illinois University. In the dining room, over the great fireplace, a motto from Edward Lear remains from the Eagle's Nest days:

"And here all these interesting animals live together in the most copious and rural harmony; seldom if anywhere else in the world is such perfect and abject happiness to be found."[174]

In 2007 residents of Oregon, Ill., located what they believe to be Taft's studio from 1902. It had been moved from the Eagle's Nest Camp in the 1930s, was remodeled and was being used as a single-car garage. A group was formed to discuss renovating it and using it as a museum to Taft and the artists' colony. The project is presently on hold.

(Above) The present garage, waiting for renovations

(Left) One of the original cabins at the camp that were turned into studios when Pond & Pond designed permanent homes

"Eternal Indian" and other Native Americans

*"The Eternal Indian" (1911) shown up close
and viewed at a distance from
the far side of the Rock River*

The camp sat on top of a bluff – "Eagle's Nest Bluff" — facing the Rock River, and the group would often make their way to the edge to watch the sun set. Hamlin Garland wrote how he demonstrated to Taft the way in which Indian chiefs would gather their robes around them.[175] Inspired by a large reinforced concrete chimney being added to the Art Institute's heating plant,[176] Taft proceeded to create a colossal figure of cast concrete on the bluff, 48 feet tall, that he called "The Eternal Indian" (1911). It now goes by the more familiar name of "Black Hawk."

Taft told a reporter:

> "I did not study any one type or race of Indians. It is a composite of the Foxes, the Sacs, the Sioux, and the Mohawks, and, in short, it represents the Indian personality. I have left off the usual Indian trappings, the feathers and buckskin and other conventional signs. There is even a hint of the old Roman in the face, which was necessary to make it suggest a spirit unconquered while still the conquered race. To be suggestive rather than direct is what I aim at – to do that is the great joy of the sculptor."[177]

A creation of this size had never before been attempted, and Taft was helped tremendously by John G. Prasuhn, a young sculptor who had become one of his assistants at the Midway Studios. In his dissertation, Williams provided this description of the process:

> "The entire camp pitched in. By mounting a scaffold upon a wagon, they searched for the most striking and effective location; the Portland Cement Company agreed to furnish the material in return for the advertising. John Prasuhn, a young engineer then living at the studios, had had experience with concrete work so, as Taft said, 'I depended absolutely on Prasuhn. My share was the six foot model.'…

> "Prasuhn constructed a vast framework of lath, chicken wire and burlap seven times the size of the working model. Hollow cast plaster sections were then hoisted and fastened into place on a timber frame which was reinforced to withstand the pressure of the concrete. The gigantic head was cast full size and lifted into position above a three-foot wide hollow tube through the center of the statue to be. Before cold weather set in, a concrete base 18 feet square was cast. All was ready by November, 1910. The cavernous interior received a spray of paraffin and clay water to prevent the mold from sticking; two tons of steel rod were built into the interior to support the massive head and to reinforce the concrete. Even though a storm had once blown down the scaffolding, it was decided to continue through the winter.

> "The weather was most uncooperative. Water for casting had to be pumped up from the river below and a heating system improvised to prevent its freezing; a vast canvas was stretched around the entire scaffold to protect it and the workers from the cold and wind. Once the casting was begun, it had to continue uninterruptedly until complete or the whole effort would fail. The water was ready, the concrete and sand waiting; casting started on December 20th. The temperature, on that exposed bluff, dropped to two below zero. Two crews of 14 men each worked around the clock in frigid weather for ten days and nights, until the vast hollow was filled to the top at 2:45 P.M., December 30th. The cast, of course, had to set before the results could be known, so the shell was left until spring.

> "Prasuhn calculated that 6,500 gallons of water, 412 barrels of Portland Cement, two tons of steel rods, 200 yards of burlap, and ten tons of plaster went into the 'Blackhawk.' Completed it stands 42 feet above the base and weighs somewhere near 268 tons.

> "No one could know whether success or abject failure would be the result before the mold was removed; the arrival of spring was most impatiently awaited that year. The first section was gingerly chipped away from the eye – the cast was perfect. The dedication ceremony which was

SIXTY-EIGHTH YEAR

SCIENTIFIC AMERICAN

THE WEEKLY JOURNAL OF PRACTICAL INFORMATION

VOLUME CVII.
NUMBER 10.

NEW YORK, SEPTEMBER 7, 1912.

10 CENTS A COPY
$3.00 A YEAR

Modeling the head in clay of the Black Hawk Statue.

HOW A HUGE STATUE OF THE AMERICAN INDIAN WAS BUILT.—[See page 192.]

(Above) Prasuhn wrote an article for Scientific American in 1912 that provided all the details of the engineering marvels involved in the creation of the "Eternal Indian." He is pictured on the cover. He wrote, "I think the most exciting time in making a statue -- and I am sure all sculptors and bronze founders will agree with me -- is the moment when the mold is about to be chopped off. Will it come out perfect or not?"

(Below) The mold is peeled back to reveal a perfectly formed mouth.

(Right) Two unidentified women pose in front of the model of the head.

(Far right) A specially designed scaffold supports the lower body as a derrick hoists the head on top.

held July 11, 1911, brought a special trainload of visitors to Oregon to hear Governor Lowden of Illinois, Edgar Bancroft, Hamlin Garland, and Taft himself speak. Except for the cement, Lorado bore all the expense of the work, cheerfully calling it 'my gift to the people of the state' – a gift that, in addition to his own time and efforts, cost over $2,500.00."[178]

Although major repairs were made to the statue in 1990-1991, it is once again in need of major restoration. It has developed cracks and areas where the surface is crumbling, and a minimum of $10,000 was needed just to pay for an expert to assess the statue's condition and outline a repair plan. In 2009 the "Eternal Indian" was listed on the National Register of Historic Places. "We need a grant to pay for the repairs. To get a grant you must be on the National

Register. It's kind of a Catch-22," said Lowden State Park site superintendent Jamie Dowdall.[179] The state has frozen its assets for such projects, so a number of private citizens are now soliciting donations to help with the repairs, now estimated at between $350,000 and $400,000. The city of Oregon, Ill., also splits the profits of an annual "Oregon Trail Days" festival with the fund-raising effort.

A plaster model of the statue is on display in the Eagle's Nest Art Colony Collection. In 2005 the library loaned the model to a local sculptor for a one-time bronze casting that stands in the entryway to Oregon's Black Hawk Center.[180] In 2009, the plaster was once again used to produce 150 small faux-bronze models sold to benefit "Oregon Trail Days" and a celebration of the statue's 100th anniversary.

Taft was also commissioned by the Paducah [Ky.] Chapter of the Daughters of the American Revolution to design a statue of Chief Paduke (1909), for whom the city was named. This piece is strikingly similar to the Native American on the side of Taft's Columbus Fountain from 1912.[181]

In 1923, Taft received a letter from the South Dakota state historian, proposing that a rock formation in the Black Hills be carved to represent "notable Sioux such as Red Cloud" and other figures symbolizing the western frontier. Taft declined the commission due to poor health. The historian then went on to contact sculptor Gutzon Borglum about the project, and Borglum suggested that subjects such as George Washington and Abraham Lincoln would arouse greater national interest in the project. The project was named after its location, "Mount Rushmore," and the rest is history.[182]

(Below) Chief Paduke (1909)

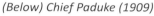

(Top) New bronze casting of the "Eternal Indian"

(Above) Native American on Columbus Fountain

Plan for Chicago's Midway Plaisance

Possibly the grandest of Taft's designs was a plan he began in 1909 to develop the mile-long green space across from his University of Chicago studio. It had been used for the "Midway" amusement park of the Columbian Exposition, and after the fair closed, the South Park commissioners had asked Frederick Law Olmsted (who had designed the fair and the University of Chicago campus) to continue his plans for developing that section. He created a parkway with a sunken center cut by four avenues, but then he died in 1903. In 1908 Taft was asked to complete Olmsted's design, and he was given two years to present a detailed plan. "This unified scheme for the decoration of the Midway I mean to make my life work," he told a reporter.[183] He envisioned a waterway running through the east-west stretch, spanned by three bridges – one each for Sciences, Arts, and Religions — decorated with busts of the world's greatest idealists.[184] Positioned at half-block intervals on either side of the waterway to tie everything together would be statues of more idealists.[185]

Taft's plan for one of the three Midway bridges

Garvey explained Taft's thought process:

> *"'It did not occur to me that I should furnish half a hundred figures for the adornment of the Midway. At most it will take fifty years to realize the plan, and I shall be neither modeling nor carving at the end of that time.' Instead, he felt the work should go to the ambitious young sculptors coming up through the ranks. His role, he explained, was only to suggest a broad scheme for improvements, which would then be implemented by those to follow."*[186]

Ada wrote: "Much to the astonishment of the good citizens of the neighborhood, Lorado even had six or eight ten-foot figures built up in staff and quietly put out one night to see how they looked!"[187]

As part of Taft's vision, at either end of the Midway, he would design a large marble fountain made up of many figures: on the west end, the "Fountain of Time," and on the east end, the "Fountain of Creation."[188]

He began crafting scale models for "Creation." The fountain's design was based on the Greek myth of Deucalion (the Noah of Greek legend) and his wife, Pyrrha. Hamlin Garland described the story behind the fountain:

> *"Deucalion and his wife, Pyrrha, being the only mortals saved by Zeus after the nine days' flood, stepped out from their frail boat on the top of Mount Parnassus, and consulted an oracle as to*

the best way of restoring the human race. They were told to cover their heads and throw the bones of their mother behind them. Pyrhha divined that these bones were the stones of Mother Earth. The monument will show us the moment when these stones cast from the Titans' hands are changing into men and women. The composition begins with creatures half-formed, vague, prostrate, blindly emerging from the shapeless rock; continues at higher level with figures fully developed and almost erect, but still groping in darkness – struggling, wondering, and wandering, until its climax is reached with an elevated group of human forms, complete and glorious, saluting the dawn."[189]

Even as Taft began revealing his plans for the Midway, people began talking about how much it would cost and what was to be depicted. The public appeared to be turning away from its appreciation of classical style sculpture and embracing a more modern art.

Roswell Field, Taft's friend and a fellow member of the Little Room, wrote a scathing piece about Taft's proposed assemblage of busts in the *Chicago Examiner*. Garvey explained:

"The novelist took Taft to task for failing to recognize how foreign his ideas were to Chicago-ans. Like others, Field challenged the sculptor's judgment in choosing heroes for his pantheon, claiming that 'local talent' like Theodore Thomas and Jane Addams were just two of many far more appropriate than the vast majority selected by Taft; the sculptor's list, Field predicted after considering the preponderance of names from antiquity, would make the Midway attractive only to 'Greek fruit peddlers and stand keepers' flocking there to glory in the 'fame and achievements of their ancestors.' …'Why should we squander our thousands and hundreds of thousands to assist in the perpetuation of the fame of men who have never heard of Chicago and who have no established genealogical or historical connection therewith? This is a poser.' …

"But Field also criticized Taft's ideas for the fountains at either end of the parkway. Basing the "Fountain of Creation" on an ancient Greek myth 'when we have a goodly number of first class myths of our own' was to the novelist inexplicable; likewise, plans to use an 'everlasting human procession' for the proposed Fountain of Time was equally mystifying when 'every schoolboy knows that creation and time, as they apply to Chicago, began back in the nineteenth century, and that real history has been humming ever since.'"[190]

Taft with full model of "Fountain of Creation," individual figures in the studio, and an enlarged photo of the model

The trustees of the Ferguson Fund said they liked Taft's Midway plan, but they agreed to fund only the "Fountain of Time." In 1913, the year his "Ferguson Fountain of the Great Lakes" was finally dedicated, he was awarded $10,000 annually over five years to complete his new monument.[191]

Ada wrote:

> "The question arises as to why the Midway plan was not carried out as a whole. Doubtless there are several reasons, but of these surely one was the fact that a new treatment of art was developing. It became the fashion to scoff at Beaux Arts methods…. With his reverence for his profession, it was disheartening later in life to find himself out of harmony with his art world, especially with its youth whom he loved so much. It might have embittered him, but his was a joyous nature, and his philosophy had ripened so that he could tolerate differences and endure disappointments."[192]

Biographer Allen Weller also tried to explain:

> "You see, to a man like Taft, the Fountain of Time, and the whole development of the Midway Plaisance, was almost a moralistic business. It was intended to make people better, more sympathetic, more understanding. This concept was simply no longer accepted in the 1920s. Art had become so personal and so individualistic that such grand public schemes just seemed impossible and out of date. So I don't think it was just a rejection of Taft personally but a change in the whole relation between art and the public which had taken place."[193]

Taft gave his own perspective to journalist John Drury:

> "I guess that was a dream that went up in smoke," he said, smiling a bit wistfully. "Chicago doesn't seem to be ready yet for such a project. Nothing has been done about it and it remains a dream – perhaps an old-fashioned dream."[194]

Even without financing, Taft continued to work on his "Fountain of Creation." When he died, nearly all of the small working models were finished, including 14 that were enlarged in plaster.[195] Walter Zimmerman used these models to sculpt individual figures in Indiana limestone (a new material for him)[196], four of which were displayed at the Century of Progress of 1933-34. One of the working models, only 12" x 4" x 6", was cast in bronze in

1934 and acquired at that time by the Brookgreen Sculpture Gardens in Murrells Inlet, S.C.; it is still on display there. Two full-scale pieces sit on the south side of the Foellinger Auditorium at the University of Illinois, and two more sculptures sit at the east entrance to the University Library.

Two completed figures of "Daughters of Pyrrha" outside the University Library (top) and two depicting "Sons of Deucalion" outside of Foellinger Auditorium

"Fountain of Time"

After many models and much thought, "The Fountain of Time" began to take shape. The trustees granting the Ferguson Fund commission required that the fountain commemorate "worthy men or women of America or important events of American history," so Taft proposed that his fountain mark the centennial of the Treaty of Ghent (1814) between Great Britain and the United States, "marking a century of perfect understanding between England and America."[197]

This work was inspired by a couplet by poet Austin Dobson, "Time goes, you say? Ah no, Alas, time stays, we go."[198] The composition would be 110 feet long and 24 feet high, with Father Time facing the group and standing some 25 feet tall. "This is the biggest undertaking I ever have considered," Taft told reporters, "but one which, of all others, I have ached to commence. It undoubtedly is the largest undertaking ever attempted in sculpture."[199] The full-scale plaster version was virtually finished in April 1917, right on schedule, when World War I broke out and its erection was postponed. It was the summer of 1920 before Taft and his assistants finally moved the monstrous mountains of plaster across the Midway to Washington Park to see how they looked.[200]

The hooded figure of Father Time faces the huge figure grouping.

Taft's original dream of sculpting this giant work in fine Georgia marble proved to be impossible.[201] "The monument had grown to be so long, so high, so complicated, that I couldn't even get a bid on the carving of it," Taft said. "I did not care to put it in bronze; my thought had been stone or something similar to stone."[202] On top of that, the Ferguson Fund had been impacted by the negative criticism that was building for Taft's Midway Plan, and they became unwilling to provide the money needed to complete the fountain in marble, granite, or bronze. However, the trustees of the Ferguson Fund could agree to fund casting of the fountain in concrete.

Taft contacted John Jacob Early, a Washington, D.C., contractor who had developed a pebble-finish architectural concrete; Early sent him samples using a buff-colored, ground quartz gravel from the Potomac River; and Taft was thrilled. "When I found I was going to get that color, like a Pointillist painting, I was more than delighted," he said. "There is not a stone that America produces – not a material, even Tennessee marble – that I would prefer...."[203]

The plaster mold into which the concrete would be cast was made up of hundreds of separate sections. The smallest were 12 inches across; the largest weighing close to 1000 pounds were about 2.5 feet by 4 feet. In all, 4500 pieces comprised what would be the largest plaster piece-mold ever made.[204] The job of casting that the Earley Studio completed in one year would have required 20 expert stone carvers to complete in the same length of time.[205]

One hundred figures, representing the journey from birth to old age, proceed in a wavelike line in front of a mysterious, hooded figure that represents Father Time. Taft explained his concept:

"The composition suggests the thought of Huxley: 'The individual drop rises and falls – the wave sweeps on.' At the right is shown the tragedy of birth, the struggle for existence, the 'survival of the fittest.' In contrast follows a sweeter note: family life, children dancing and young girls. The religious motif is illustrated by monks, nuns and ecstatics in distinctive costumes. A poet setting out to conquer the world makes an eager gesture. In the center, seated on an armored horse and surrounded by soldiers with floating banners, refugees and camp followers, rides the conqueror. From this height in the composition the waves gradually diminish again. Temporary power as typified in the conqueror is shown as of relatively little importance in the eyes of Father Time. The three young girls in the foreground were at first thought of as three fates or furies of the battlefield, but later took shape as the spirit of youth peering forward and trying to outstrip the current of life itself. The remaining waves of the front show groups of lovers, old age, a dancing girl who indulges in a last burst of merriment near the brink of the unknown, and the last wave shows the young man, resisting as youth does the power of death, while the final figure, an old man, welcomes death with outstretched arms, as a release and a fulfillment."[206]

What Taft didn't mention was that he included himself in the figures, on the back, west side of the sculpture, rather than signing the piece. He wears an artist's smock and appears to be meditating as he walks with hands clasped behind him. Behind him walks his janitor, Jellsomeno.[207] A granite arrow in the ground points to them.

Herbert George, professor emeritus of sculpture at the University of Chicago, presented a program on the "Fountain of Time" as part of a 1991 Humanities Open House in Chicago. A reporter relayed George's analysis of the composition:

> "'What's the basic configuration of this piece?' George asks. 'You've seen it before. Here…' He pulls a sheet of paper from his pocket and unfolds it. It is a drawing of a classic Greek pediment, the figures ascending and descending within a triangle, with the single figure – in this case, the goddess Athena – placed at the apex.

> "'Taft was in love with Greek sculpture,' George continues, 'but he's also departing from that tradition to make a fascinating point He takes the central figure of the piece – which is Time – and removes it from the pediment, turning it around so that it's looking back at humanity. And who is Time opposed by? Who is up there in his place? The general on the horse. What was the date when Taft completed this piece? 1922. The world has passed through the most horrific war in recent memory, the war to end all wars, supposedly. So that figure dominates, and Taft places Time in opposition to it.'"[208]

The "Fountain of Time" was officially dedicated on November 15, 1922, nearly 14 years after Taft conceived of the project. A review of Taft's finished product in a 1926 *Chicago Tribune* called it one of the city's "pet

atrocities," and wrote that the curving row of white figures looked like false teeth smiling across the end of the Midway.[209] It called the work "hopelessly pretentious and inappropriate. … Like a stripped fighter, Chicago is beautiful when it doesn't mean to be. No city can surpass it. But when Chicago tries, 'dolls up' and decorates, the result too often is sad, if not atrocious."[210]

Eighty years later Alan Artner, art columnist for the *Chicago Tribune*, would write that "No other work of public art in Chicago matches the symbolic grandeur of Taft's Fountain of Time."[211]

Chicago's weather conditions were not kind to "Time" and its 9000-square-foot reflecting pool, designed by Howard Van Doren Shaw. The city's winters, pollution, and possibly acid rain created numerous cracks, chips, and holes that ran along the entire length of the structure.[212] "Lorado should have gone to Paris and built the thing there," wrote *Chicago Tribune* columnist Bill Granger. "It might be indoors now, in a place like the restored train station in Paris that houses great works of the 19th century, where it would be protected from the elements. They do that in places like Paris and Florence and Rome…."[213]

Jeff Huebner, writing in the *Chicago Reader*, detailed the deterioration:

> "Beginning in the mid-'30s, attempts began to repair the structure. … Additional repairs were made in the mid-'50s and again in the '60s; Mayor Richard J. Daley rededicated the monument in 1966. Each time the crews patched cracks with concrete that was a different color and more rigid than the original, and the sculpture just cracked again when the seasons changed. They also sandblasted the work to clean it, stripping off details and some of the aggregate coating. By the 1980s the main portion of the sculpture was in the worst shape of any of the 100 or so artworks on Park District property. Some details had been lost altogether, the interior was

Taft included his own smocked figure on the back side of the fountain, second from right.

(Right) A granite marker in the grass indicates his location.

crumbling because of moisture buildup, and the smooth buff-colored surface had become rough and drab. This monument to transience was itself succumbing to time. 'It was almost completely past the point of ever being saved,' says Herbert George. 'It was going to be bulldozed if they'd left it there.'"[214]

In 1983, the Ferguson Fund (the same entity that had originally funded the creation of the sculpture) once again came into the picture, hiring a consulting firm to assess the damage and estimate the cost of repairs. In 1984 the trustees rejected a full-scale restoration program because they couldn't afford the $376,000 price tag.[215] For three winters in the late 1980s, workers covered the piece with a huge plastic tarp to protect it from further damage. In 1989, the consultants were retained again; this time they outlined a preliminary budget of $450,000; and this time the Ferguson Fund, the Park District, and the University of Chicago worked out a plan to share the cost. (The University of Chicago later backed out of its commitment.)[216] But in the late 1990s restoration actually began.

The restoration was led by Andrzej Dajnowski, who had been a conservator at the Smithsonian Institution. He had the input of concrete consultants, an architectural firm, and Barbara Hall, the Art Institute's senior objects conservator. After stabilizing the main sculpture to prevent further damage, they cleaned and dried out the hollow interior, then installed a ventilation system to stop moisture from building up again. They replaced drainpipes, added new beams and columns, reinforced corroded steel rebars, and used concrete to strengthen the upper levels. By 1997 the internal work was done. Then Dajnowski (who in the meantime had formed his own company) went on to repair and resurface the main sculpture and the figure of Father Time. A two-story shed was built around the procession section, which would allow the conservators to work in any weather.

"Dajnowski and his crew of ten began work in early 1999. They spent nearly a year cleaning the surface and removing loose material and the old patches. Cracks that ran deep beneath the surface were left because they allowed the sculpture to expand, but surface cracks and holes were filled. The crew also installed a 'moving joint' system that Dajnowski designed, which involved placing titanium rods and wires in the eight or nine largest cracks that had opened up on their own. … By the summer of 2001 they were gearing up for the most demanding task – 'parging,' or hand-brushing, a thin coat of concrete slurry containing buff-colored gravel and cement onto the sculpture's 103 figures and using another mix to restore about two dozen missing or severely eroded details. 'There were some creases of cloth, some fingers, a gesture, a soldier's sword or scabbard, a face where there had to be some emotion brought back,' says Jones. 'It wasn't just schmearing concrete.'"[217]

The procession was finished by the end of the summer of 2001, and "Father Time" was finished in November. The total bill came to $1.23 million.

But the reflecting pool remained unfinished until 2005. Previous inspection had revealed that it needed work as well, so the concrete around the basin and below the ground was removed and replaced; new sewer and water lines were put in; and the entire bottom of the pool was redone, for an additional cost of $845,000.[218] On August 18, 2007, Chicago's mayor, Richard J. Daley, presided over another rededication of the "Fountain of Time" and its reflecting basin. All that was left to complete was $150,000' worth of lighting. As of 2012, the pool is filled, but there is still no night illumination.

(Clockwise, from top)
The protective scaffold and covering are erected.
Previous patching to be replaced.
The monk's surface before and after.

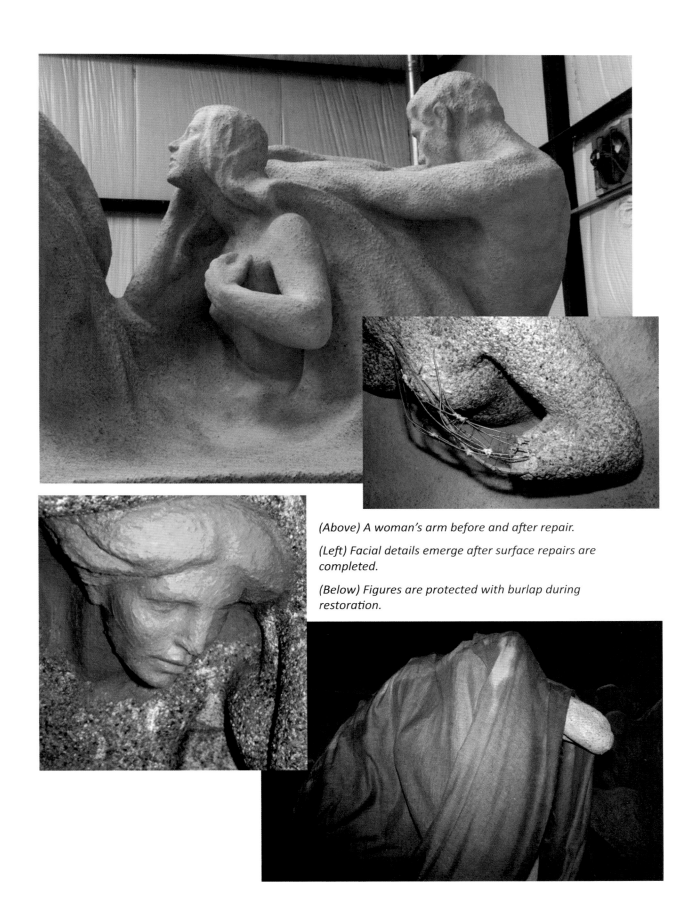

(Above) A woman's arm before and after repair.

(Left) Facial details emerge after surface repairs are completed.

(Below) Figures are protected with burlap during restoration.

Details from "The Fountain of Time"

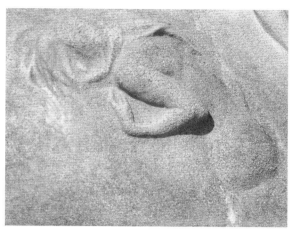

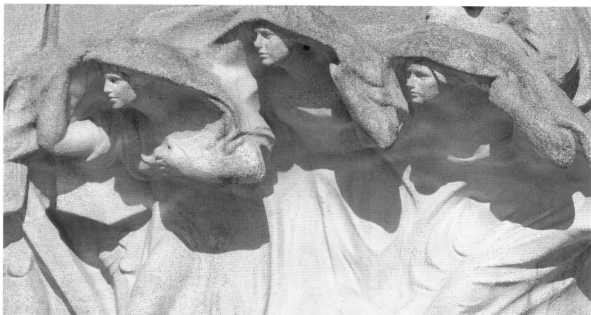

The Elmwood "Pioneers"

By 1925, Lorado Taft was practically a household name, and residents of his hometown of Elmwood, bursting with pride, contacted him to create a sculpture just for them. An agreement was reached: If the town could raise $15,000 for the casting and the base mounting, Taft would donate his work. After five very active months, $17,589.40 was raised or had been pledged. "The Pioneers," weighing some 3,500 pounds and standing ten feet tall, arrived in a railroad boxcar, and a monument company provided a four-foot-high granite base.[219]

This strongly crafted image of a man, woman and child, and dog, looks out across the prairie, and the inscription reads: "To the pioneers who bridged the streams, subdued the soil and founded a state." Weller explained that Taft's gift to Elmwood was "a contribution to the adornment of the community [and was] an act of primary importance to him."[220]

"The statue was unveiled on Sunday, May 27, 1928. Two thousand invitations had been mailed, and Civil War veterans were given special seating. The day was sunny and cool. Visitors came by train and car. Streets, stores, and houses were decorated. The Elmwood Hotel advertised chicken dinners for $1. Bleachers were set up, and a sound system was in place. Many brought lunch baskets and made a day-long picnic. The Taft party arrived in time for services at the nearby Congregational Church, where Lorado's father had been headmaster of the Elmwood Academy 73 years earlier. After the service, dinner was served at the church. At 1:30 the Elmwood Band began a concert. An estimated 5,000 to 10,000 people were present by this time. A squad of Peoria motorcycle policemen was present, directed by Mr. C.A. Vance. There was an invocation by Rev. J.W. Turner of the Methodist Church, the grade school chorus sang, and Dr. Robert E. Hieronymous from the University of Illinois told of the work that had been done to arrive at the dedication. Mrs. Marian Brown Pollitz, daughter of the E.L. Browns, and Miss Emily Taft, Lorado's daughter – who later married U.S. Senator Paul Douglas – pulled the veil aside to show everyone The Pioneers. Mayor S.R. Fleisher officially accepted the statue. Songs were sung, telegrams were read, and the University of Illinois president, Dr. David McKinley, added his congratulations. Taft greeted the people, and his brother-in-law, noted author Hamlin Garland, gave the principal address. Across the street, an eight-grade boy by the name of Danny Maher did a brisk business selling hamburgers."[221]

"The Pioneers" was added to the National Register of Historic Places in 2001, which makes Elmwood even prouder.

(Right) The plaster model for the "Pioneers," painted bronze, stands beneath a stairway in the Library Building of the University of Illinois.

(Facing page) The bronze version (1928) standing in Elmwood's town square

TO THE PIONEERS
WHO BRIDGED THE STREAMS
SUBDUED THE SOIL AND
FOUNDED A STATE

"Alma Mater"

Taft was very fond of his alma mater, the University of Illinois, and in 1929 completed a sculptural grouping that now stands in front of Altgeld Hall at the corner of Green and Wright streets in Urbana. (Taft began thinking about creating this sculpture as early as 1883.)[222] The figures originally stood on the south side of the Auditorium because the facility was located in the center of the campus. The sculpture was moved to its present location at Green and Wright streets in 1962.

The female figure, "Alma Mater," wears the seal of the university on her gown, and she is flanked by a male and a female figure depicting "Learning" and "Labor" (words contained on the university's official seal). The cost of the actual fabrication was provided by a series of class gifts, but Taft contributed all of his own work on this monumental piece, and he was awarded an honorary doctorate when the group was dedicated on the 50th anniversary of his graduation.[223] Graduates fondly remember this sculptural grouping, and its image appears on stationery and other items, including porcelain plates.

Edmund Janes James, who was president of the University from 1904 to 1920, once told a committee of the state legislature, "If the University of Illinois had never done anything more than to produce Lorado Taft, it would have justified all of the millions that the State has expended in its upbuilding and maintenance."[224] When Taft died, the *University Alumni News* called him "the University's most famous son."[225]

"Alma Mater" was one of many strong females that Taft would sculpt over his lifetime. In his dissertation, Williams described the unique style of Taft's women:

"Taft's classic-allegoric female figure … tends to be less ideal and more human – more like a healthy Midwestern girl than a Greek goddess. She is less renaissance than those of French and Saint-Gaudens; less animated than MacMonnies'; and much less a mere academic cliché than such figures often turned out to be…."[226]

Workmen prepare to move "Alma Mater" to her new location at Green and Wright streets.

*The University of Illinois' beloved figure grouping of "Alma Mater"
(completed in 1929) now stands in front of Altgeld Hall.
The female figure (inset) wears the seal of the university on her gown. The
inscription reads: "To thy happy children of the future
those of the past send greetings."*

The University of Illinois has reciprocated Taft's affections. Taft's papers are housed in the University's archives, and a complete listing of these materials is available online.[227] One of the campus streets is named "Taft Drive," and one of the residence halls bears his name. In 1981 the family house was cut in half and moved onto campus, to 1401 South Maryland, when the original lot was selected as a new location for the Swanlund Administration Building; it was remodeled and now serves as office space.

Alma Mater to be moved for off-site conservation efforts
INSIDE ILLINOIS, Feb. 16, 2012 | Christian Gollayan, News Bureau Intern

This summer, pedestrians near Wright and Green streets may notice that something is missing. After commencement, the spot that's been home to the 82-year-old Alma Mater sculpture since 1962 will be vacant and the campus icon may not return for nearly a year.

Yearlong absence
The Alma Mater Group sculpture will be moved off-campus after commencement to begin what could be a yearlong treatment plan to repair the effects of years of neglect.

"We have stipulated that it be back on its base before May 4, 2013, because it's a popular spot for graduation photos," said Melvyn Skvarla, the campus historic preservation officer.

Since its dedication in 1929, the sculpture has gone decades without proper maintenance and is now literally deteriorating at the seams. Funded by the Office of the Chancellor, the UI's Preservation Working Group had been seeking a private firm for the Alma Mater conservation project.

Conservation of Sculpture and Objects Studio Inc., of Forest Park, Ill., was recently approved to repair the sculpture for $99,962. At the end of the semester, the firm will move the sculpture from its base to the company's 13,000-square-foot facility. Staff conservators will examine the sculpture more closely and then develop and implement a conservation treatment plan.

The studio will decide how to disassemble and move the sculpture. Most likely, Skvarla said, the sculpture will be taken apart in two sections and lifted onto a flatbed truck with a crane. There has been no decision yet to put in place a temporary sculpture. For now, according to Skvarla, plans call for the base to be empty. Unlike small sculptures that are cast in one piece, the Alma Mater sculpture was cast in at least 30 sections and then bolted together.

Although sculptor Lorado Taft wanted students to celebrate his Alma Mater sculpture by climbing on it, the sculpture is in such a degraded condition that "she could actually be seriously damaged if someone were to climb on her at this point," said Jennifer Hain Teper, a conservation librarian and chair of the Preservation Working Group. |

Sculptor Lorado Taft intended for students to climb on the sculpture and celebrate it. Over the years, however, this has produced cracks in the arms, backs and necks of the three figures.

"She could actually be seriously damaged if someone were to climb on her at this point," said Jennifer Hain Teper, a conservation librarian and chair of the Preservation Working Group. "(The restoration) will strengthen the interior (of the sculpture) so it can stand another hundred years or more," Skvarla said.

The sculpture's last major repair was done in 1981 by Robert Youngman, a university sculpture professor. Youngman and his team strengthened the internal armatures, replaced the rusted steel bolts, sprayed the pieces with a rust inhibitor and caulked the statue's joints

According to Skvarla, some of these repairs may have caused internal damage. "If you caulk everything, the water can't get out," Skvarla said. "So therefore it's rusting from the inside — oxidizing — and that creates problems."

Large areas of the sculpture are exhibiting uneven surface corrosion. Alma's face is streaked in green patina — tarnish caused by oxidizing copper. Parts of her throne are splotched in white and black. Skvarla said that the corrosion was caused by natural environmental action, air pollution (exhaust fumes from vehicles) and defacement by pedestrians.

Once the sculpture is off site, the studio will disassemble the Alma Mater to examine the extent of the damage and perform a chemical analysis of the sculpture's surface corrosion. After presenting this information to the university, the conservator will perform the necessary repairs.

"(The restoration) will strengthen the interior (of the sculpture) so it can stand another hundred years or more," said Skvarla.

The Office of the Chancellor has agreed to maintain the sculpture after the conservation project is complete. The sculpture will receive a power washing and hot waxing at least once every three years to prevent corrosion.

Currently, the university has not decided whether the sculpture will be restored to its natural bronze color or whether it will be made to appear green again.

As part of the contract, the conservator will present three lectures reporting on the status of the project. The first will be about the sculpture's condition and proposed treatment plan. Midway into the conservation project, a second lecture will discuss what has been done to date. After the project is complete, the final lecture will reveal the final steps of the process and a proposed maintenance plan.

"In addition," Teper said, "there are a lot of students on campus in the art program and library science program who are interested in the profession of conservation. We're hoping to use this as a learning experience for these students as well."

While some may miss the statue's green streaks (if it is decided to restore the sculpture to its original color) and long for the nostalgia of her caulked joints, Skvarla said that people will learn to embrace the change in the statue's renovated appearance.

"It's just like when they cleaned the buildings at the Louvre," Skvarla said. "They were a dirty black limestone and when they cleaned them and they were white, people were first startled but eventually they liked it.

"And so (with the Alma Mater), you get used to seeing it one way, but that's not really the authentic way it was when it was at its high point."

Chicago's Century of Progress

Taft was in his 70s when the Great Depression hit, and major commissions were few and far between. In 1933, the city of Chicago optimistically hosted the Century of Progress International Exposition, and Taft was commissioned to create the 20-foot-tall figure of "Justice" for the United States Government Building.

Weller explained that "Lee Lawrie was appointed director of sculpture and, in addition to his own work, major pieces were created by Ulric Ellerhusen, Leo Friedlander, Alfonso Iannelli, Raoul Josset, Gaston Lachaise, John Storrs, Louise Lentz Woodruff, and Lorado Taft. Taft was by far the oldest artist of this group, and the only sculptor of his generation who was given a major commission. Three of these sculptors had been his students."[228] Midway Studios, once employing dozens of assistants, was down to a total staff of six.[229]

"Come Unto Me" was a large, 14-foot-tall low relief panel Taft created for the exposition's Hall of Religions, recreating a painting by Danish artist Karl Heinrich Bloch. When the building and its decoration were slated for demolition, J.L. Kraft (president of what became Kraft Foods) retrieved the panel and installed it in Chicago's North Shore Baptist Church, where he was a parishioner. Sturdier than it appears, it has survived two moves: one from the fair to the church, and a second from the original church to a new building.

Biographer Weller wrote:

"It was only now in old age and for probably purely financial reasons that [Taft] agreed to translate the composition of a painting into low relief. Photographs of Bloch's painting suggest that Taft's copy is far more interesting than the original. In very low relief, the plaster is finished with an ivory-like surface with a gold background. Few people would recognize it as Taft's work; it has never been properly cited and remains almost unknown.... It has the same kind of uniform, simplified surface as the grave monument "The Crusader."[230]

(Left) The 20-foot-tall figure of "Justice" at the Century of Progress Exposition (1933) has since been destroyed.

(Opposite page) The large plaster bas relief of "Come Unto Me" (1933) was moved from a previous church to its present location with no damage.

(Inset) The original painting by Karl Heinrich Bloch.

Louisiana's State Capitol

That same year, 1933, Taft also designed two groups, each approximately 14 feet tall, for the new state capitol building at Baton Rouge, La.: "The Patriots" (with a large armored knight standing on the coffin of a fallen hero) and "The Pioneers" (featuring a woman representing the spirit of Adventure).

Vincent Kubly provided details in his book, *The Louisiana Capitol: Its Art and Architecture:*[231]

Architect Weiss explained the significance of the two groups in the following terms: The west buttress group, the "Pioneers," is a tribute to the founders of Louisiana, who with fortitude explored and inhabited the valley and overcame the forces of man and nature through the early periods of its development. The French and Spanish explorers and colonists of the seventeenth and eighteenth centuries, the Indians who were the original inhabitants of this region, and the American, who, attracted by the fertility of the land and the advantages of location of this section of the country, came here to found homes and farms and to establish commercial enterprises – to the great soldiery of peace, and to statesmanship.

The east buttress group, the "Patriots," is a memorial to those Louisianians, of heterogeneous nationalities, who shed their blood in defense of their homes and in the establishment of their liberties; who fought to repel the usurper and the foreign foe; who, under great strategists and leaders, such as Gen. Andrew Jackson, set boldly the name of Louisiana and of New Orleans upon the pages of history, and contributed their portion in accomplishing the solidarity of the Union of American states. And in the group there is expressed the sorrows of war, depicted in the piteous figures of the mother and father, the widow and the orphan, of the armed defender. This group is dedicated to the brave soldiery of war, to militant patriotism.

The Pioneer group is dominated by a large "dreamy-eyed woman" personifying the Spirit of Adventure, who stands atop a pair of iron-bound treasure chests. At her feet the various fruits and vegetables that grow in Louisiana lie on the chest. The figures grouped around the treasure chests and allegorical figure are led by the explorers De Soto and La Salle, representing the Spanish and French who first came to the area. Two missionary priests following these explorers hold an open Bible over the symbolic treasure. The hooded monk behind De Soto represents the Franciscan friars who followed in the wake of the Spanish explorers to convert savage natives to Christianity, while the priest to the rear of La Salle may be a representation of the Jesuit Father Hennepin, who accompanied him on some of his explorations. Behind these figures is a picturesque entourage composed of a frontiersman in buckskins and a coonskin cap, a Spanish conquistador, French settlers, and Indians.

The central figure of the Patriot group is an armored knight standing over the coffin of a fallen hero, which is surrounded by a group of mourners. On the bier are a wreath and a palm, symbols of mourning and sacrifice. The mourners are led by an aged couple and a man holding his hat over his heart, conveying the ideas of bereavement and lamentation quite expressively. The other mourners in the procession are rather stereotyped, less varied than the Pioneers, owing to the nature of the subject. [232]

Williams provided further details of the Baton Rouge commission in his dissertation:

"The commission turned out to be a rather unhappy one for Taft. There were disagreements from the start: that renowned art critic, Huey Long, even objected to part of the design, and the architects were in a tremendous hurry. To climax the whole, Taft was stricken with illness and was unable to finish the work to his own satisfaction, even with valiant help from his assistants. Both 20-foot groups were in plaster and out of the studio within a year as per contract, the last being shipped in April, 1932. Displeased with the way the pieces were being carved in stone on location, the sculptor finally sent, at his own expense, his own stone-cutter to finish the carving. He wrote the architects that the whole business was 'a catastrophe … but will rush. I shall make nothing on it, but it has kept my people busy.' A few days later,

"The Patriots" (far left) and "The Pioneers" flank the entrance to the Louisiana Capitol.

Taft added, 'I resent models being chopped out in a couple of months. I thought I had been invited to do something permanent. It has been impossible.'[233]

When compared with Taft's figure groupings created for the entrance to the Horticulture Building at the Columbian Exposition of 1893, the groups of figures at the entrance to the Baton Rouge capitol building showed a remarkable change in his style. Williams explained:

"Both were pylon compositions placed on each side of a main entrance of an imposing building. While the Fair figures had an almost baroque restlessness, the Baton Rouge forms are quiet and calm; a rather naturalistic figure type has changed into simplified generalizations of the human form; realist detail, in the earlier, has disappeared to be replaced by clean shapes and surfaces; the later composition has in depth and linear organization an ease and clarity lacking in the Fair groups. These two works from almost the time extremes of Taft's production, shared a feeling of aptness to the style of the buildings on which they were located, and looked well in place...."[234]

Taft placed the figure of a young mother and her baby on the back side of the "Pioneer" group, as if they are sitting on a covered wagon, heading west to a new home.

Nearing the end

aft's health had been failing for some time. High blood pressure was discovered in 1919, and he was constantly troubled by sciatica. In July 1931 he had been afflicted with an embolism that left him bedridden for two weeks. And in 1932 he had undergone prostate surgery.[235] "Mr. Taft had been suffering from heart disease for several years," reported the *Chicago Daily News*, "and his physicians had warned him time and again that he should let up a little in his work and his friends had urged him to take a vacation to conserve his health. This, however, he refused to do. He was active to the last...."[236]

In 1936 he traveled to Quincy, Ill., for the 78th anniversary of the sixth great debate between Abraham Lincoln and Stephen Douglas – his last public appearance – where his latest commission, a monument depicting the

(Above) Taft's bronze depiction of the Lincoln-Douglas Debate (1936) stands in the park where the sixth great debate took place.

(Right) The full-size painted plaster model is on display at the College of Law at the University of Illinois.

Don Carlos Taft

debate, was positioned on the exact spot in Washington Park where the debate took place. A crowd estimated at 10,000 to 12,000 attended to see the unveiling of the piece, which measures approximately eight feet tall, nine feet wide, and a foot thick. Taft died a few weeks after.

Just 20 days before he died, he presented a bust of his father to the village of Elmwood. He had created it many years earlier and had brought it back for final changes. It now stands in the Elmwood Public Library.

On his deathbed, Taft showed concern that he would be unable to complete another piece in progress, of George Washington, Haym Solomon, and Robert Morris, which honored the two bankers who largely financed the American Revolution. It was commissioned by Chicago lawyer Barnet Hodes. One newspaper reported, "When Taft was assured by members of his staff of coworkers that they would faithfully carry out his plans, he said, 'Now I can die happy.'" Taft's associates at the Midway Studios — Nellie Walker, Mary Webster, and Leonard Crunelle – each enlarged one of the figures, and the finished work was dedicated in 1941. "The students' product was so like Taft's work that only experts could detect any slight variations in style," wrote one journalist.[237] Moved from its original location at Heald Square, it now stands at the edge of Wacker Drive and the Chicago River in downtown Chicago, and in 1971 it was the first monument designated by the Chicago City Council as a sculptural landmark.[238] Harry Barnard wrote a book in 1971 about the subject and the sculpture entitled *This Great Triumvirate of Patriots.*[239]

(Above) A spectacular bronze panel of "Lady Liberty," surrounded by thousands of detailed figures, is mounted on the reverse side of the base.

(Right) The grouping of Washington, Solomon, and Morris was completed by Taft's associates in 1941.

MORRIS GEORGE WASHINGTON

Krannert Art Museum Exhibition

The Krannert Art Museum at the University of Illinois at Urbana-Champaign possesses, without a doubt, the largest collection of Lorado Taft's work. At last count, they have 176 pieces.[240] In the winter of 1983 they mounted a retrospective exhibition – the first and only survey of Taft's art. It featured 19 portrait busts, 15 other works, and 38 sketches and studies. Allen Weller brought the material together, some of it never seen before. He also wrote the catalog essay. The Illinois Arts Council also made available its photographs of Taft's monuments and provided a grant to support the show. Without Weller, who died in 1997, it is unlikely that such an exhibition will ever again be mounted.

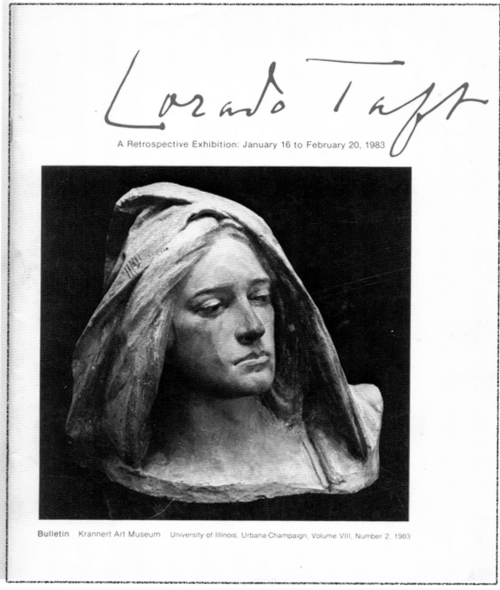

Lorado Taft

A Retrospective Exhibition: January 16 to February 20, 1983

Bulletin   Krannert Art Museum   University of Illinois, Urbana-Champaign, Volume VIII, Number 2, 1983

*The Krannert exhibition of Taft's work included this "Ideal Head" from 1910-15,
a work in plaster that is 20 inches high. Allen Weller, curator of the show, hypothesized that it
may have been created to be part of the work Taft used in his public lectures. [241]*

"The Blind"

The members of the Eagle's Nest Colony spent long hours creating, and they would often relax by reading plays and excerpting parts to perform. Taft unearthed a copy of Maurice Maeterlinck's *Les Aveugles (The Blind)* and translated it from French into English. In the story, a group of sightless people, of different ages and types, are led on a walk by an ancient sighted priest who dies on the trip. A mother holds her baby high in the hope that he will see light and be able to help them find their way home.

Mr. Taft stated:

> "After I had read the play, that wonderful tragedy whose symbolism expressed the great longing of all humanity for light in life, the group shaped itself in my dreams. It refused to vanish, and as it exhibited the concentration of a powerful emotion within the canons of sculptural composition, I made a small model to see how it would appear in the clay. … It does not point to the hopeless note of Maeterlinck at the close. The hope that a little child shall lead them is one that all gladly accept as it keeps alive the light of faith that the race renews itself in young. It was a greatly absorbing creation. I felt for them, I experienced the deepest emotion while modeling the faces of the blind. The pathos of the helpless individual in the posture of the figures, the hands reaching upward into empty air, appealing to the great God above for guidance."[242]

Taft recreated this lost group into a 40-inch-long plaster sculpture, and this maquette is now on display in the Eagle's Nest Art Colony Collection in Oregon. In 2007, to celebrate the 100th anniversary of modeling of the statue, Oregon resident Betty M.E. Croft, representing the Art Committee of the Oregon Public Library, recruited fellow residents to pose for a tableau vivant of "The Blind" and to read from Taft's translation.

The plaster maquette of "The Blind" (1907) at the Eagle's Nest Gallery in Oregon, Ill.

(Left) The bronze casting of "The Blind" finally took place in 1988.

(Inset) Members of the tableau vivant staged in Oregon, Ill., for the 100th anniversary of the modeling of the statue.

An even larger plaster version, measuring approximately 10.5 feet long, 9 feet tall, and 6 feet wide was included in three important exhibitions in 1908 in Chicago, Baltimore, and New York.[243]

Taft was never able to find a patron who would make it possible to cast the piece in bronze, and the plaster stood in the Midway Studios during Taft's lifetime. After he died, the University of Illinois brought it from the studios and installed it in their Architecture Building. Later it was moved to the lobby of the University Auditorium, where it was neglected and even vandalized, and finally it was put in storage. In 1973, professor Robert Youngman, a sculptor on the staff of the School of Art and Design, began making a technical examination of the work and preparing recommendations concerning its condition and future. He discovered that the piece actually consisted of 23 separate plaster sections connected by steel bolts. In 1975 the sculpture was moved to a large warehouse where Youngman and his two daughters stripped layers of paint from the surfaces and repaired and strengthened many damaged sections.

But then the statue moved again, in 1982, to the basement of Smith Music Hall where it remained for five years. Finally, in 1988, a donor came forward to pay for the casting in bronze – the Estate of William S. Kinkead – and the piece moved once again, this time to a sculpture foundry in New Jersey. Using photos from the University Archives, along with additional photos of Oregon's smaller version, workers continued with the repairs on the plaster statue. Missing pieces were reproduced and reattached – 13 hands, three heads, five different body parts, and one walking staff were recreated in this manner. After the repairs were carefully completed, molds were made: 33 for the upper part and 11 for the bottom section. Then, after casting, the sections were positioned together and welded and a patina was applied. The piece was installed in the fall of 1988 in the Kinkead Pavilion, an addition to the Krannert Art Museum designed specifically to house the sculpture. This is indeed a success story that ranks up there with the restoration of the "Fountain of Time."[244]

"Orpheus Consoled" remains!

At the same time that Taft was completing the "Fountain of Time," he was commissioned by Thomas Edison's employees to create a sculpture for Edison's 75th birthday, Feb. 11, 1922. "Orpheus Consoled" depicts the Greek god Orpheus, son of Apollo and the muse Calliope, who could play the lyre so beautifully that angry people and wild beasts were soothed, and rocks and streams could be charmed. It is said that the oak trees growing along the coast of Thrace migrated there to better hear Orpheus's songs. So Taft bent the myth slightly, showing Orpheus discarding his lyre and instead lifting a phonograph record. The statue went on display in Edison's library in Menlo Park, N.J., and has not moved since then. The library, now a part of the Edison National Historic Site, recently has gone through a major renovation, and Orpheus continues to sit in a place of honor.

The Edison Library has undergone a major renovation, but the figure of "Orpheus Consoled" (1922) still sits in its original position against the wall, shown in this vintage photo.

Mysteries solved ...

The Lorado Taft archives include mention of an "Ella McGuinness" memorial, with the location listed as Indianapolis. Glory-June Greiff, who authored a book on Indiana outdoor sculpture for the Indiana Historical Society,[245] did not list this piece in her research. However, she also happened to volunteer as a docent at Indianapolis's Crown Hill Cemetery, and she knew of a memorial to "Mary Ella McGinnis" that was among visitors' favorites. Although the cemetery didn't know who the sculptor was, they listed the delicate little marble statue in the "Notable Persons" section of their website, along with Benjamin Harrison, James Whitcomb Riley, Jefferson Davis, and John Dillinger.[246] By matching up the correspondence and photographs in the archives with the actual memorial, we now know that Mary Ella McGinnis had died in 1875 at the age of 5, and her mother commissioned Taft to sculpt the piece as a surprise for her father, Civil War general George McGinnis. Mary Ella can be found in Section 16: the beautiful young girl holding an apron full of flowers, with her hair in long ringlets.

Mary Ella McGinnis (1888)

Pieces we can't see ...

In 1914, Taft was asked by the Infant Welfare Society to create a figure of a mother and child to serve as the visual symbol of the society. His design, some 15 inches tall and 14 inches wide, was unveiled for "Babies Week in Chicago," and 50 copies of the design were created. (The Lorado Taft Museum in Elmwood has one of these copies.)

A bronze casting wasn't made until 1961, to celebrate the society's golden jubilee year, and for the event society members decided "to do something to preserve the figures for everyone's enjoyment." They presented the

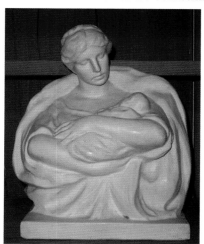

bronze to the Art Institute. "It's fitting that this statue should be a part of the permanent collection of the Art Institute, which serves the cultural needs of Chicago as we endeavor to serve the city's health needs," said Hartley Laycock, Jr., as he made the presentation. The bronze, resting on a brick pedestal, was "permanently" installed in the walled garden adjoining the Decorative Arts gallery, until it was moved inside and put in storage.[247]

In 1977, the society asked the Art Institute if they could have the piece back to display it at the Philip D. Armour Child & Family Center, but their request was declined. As of 2012, it still sits in storage.

The earliest versions of the Infant Welfare Society figure of a mother and child were cast out of a substance called "ivorine."

And new discoveries …

An unusual art find – what may be the final sculpture of Lorado Taft – resurfaced on eBay in 2009 after more than 50 years in private hands. The 14-1/2-inch-high bronze figure of a man – young, with face and arms upraised – is called "Aspiration."

It was made to be a sketch model for a 10-foot marble memorial statue for the grave of Emmons McCormick Blaine, Jr., who died of pneumonia in 1918 at the age of 28, but the actual piece was never completed. Taft was at work on a larger plaster working model, about five feet tall, when he died in 1936.

Photographs of Taft's studio at the time of his death show the larger version of the sculpture plus the smaller version and a plaster maquette. Taft historians assume that the larger piece was destroyed, but the small statue probably was given to Blaine's mother and disposed of by trustees of her estate after she died in 1954. The statue showed up in 1955 in a Chicago antique shop, where it was purchased by Thomas McDonough and his wife. They made inquiries to art experts and persons who had known Taft to confirm that it was in fact an original piece. Mary Webster, who had been Taft's assistant and secretary, knew of the piece and that it had been cast in bronze by the Gorham Foundries, but she had not seen it again.[248]

Oregon resident Betty M.E. Croft purchased the statue on eBay and then generously donated it to the Eagle's Nest Art Colony Collection.

"Aspiration" is shown above in the Eagle's Nest Art Colony Collection and below in two plaster versions in Taft's studio (see the small model far right). It was never completed in marble.

Exciting plans for the future.

Travis Ross, visualization laboratory manager at the Beckman Institute of the University of Illinois, performed a 3D scan of Lorado Taft's low-relief sculpture of Katharine Lucinda Sharp in July of 2011. The final 3D image was created by stitching together 40 individual scans, each capturing the rich texture of a piece that was originally sculpted in 1921.

John Unsworth, dean of the university's Graduate School of Library and Information Science, requested the scan of the piece that hangs in the university library. "We're grateful to the Imaging Technology Group and the Library for helping us turn Katharine Sharp into information that can now be shared freely," he said.[249]

"This project is very exciting for us," explains Mr. Ross. "3D images can be used to create reproductions that museums could loan out rather than risk damage to the original. They can be used to create models in all sizes and materials so more people may be able to see the great artworks of the world for themselves. They will be the archives for future generations.

"They could be used to create virtual reality exhibitions on your smartphone -- just scan a bar code, the image will download, and you can take it home.

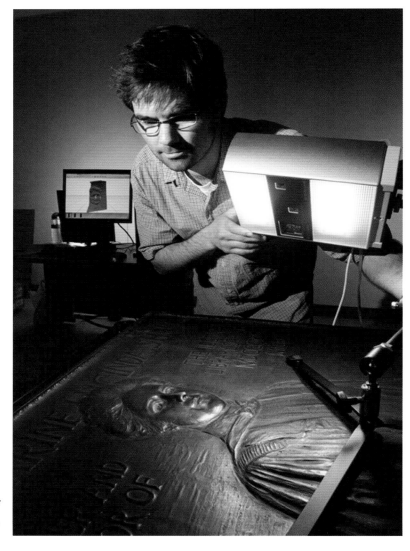

"And in the footsteps of Lorado Taft, they also can be used as the models to repair and conserve damaged objects. We could scan broken individual pieces and do virtual assembly.

"Here at the Beckman Institute, we can use the scan data to build a duplicate for a fraction of what it would have cost to produce commercially. We created the 3D image of the Katharine Sharp plaque in only a couple days," Ross says. "Now that we have 'practiced' and we have new, state-of-the-art scanners, we're ready to create 3D images of all kinds of art ... or anything!"

Can you imagine a 3D image of Taft's "Fountain of Time" in its own room in a museum?

Travis Ross scans Taft's plaque of Katharine Sharp to prepare a 3D image.

Taft's death and gravesite

Taft died on October 30, 1936, at his Chicago home. He had suffered a stroke while working on "Aspiration" in his studio, and he died several days later. Funeral services were held in his studio on Saturday, October 31. Later, a memorial service for Taft was held in Rockefeller Chapel on the University of Chicago campus. On December 10, his ashes were scattered in the Elmwood Township Cemetery near the grave of his aunt, Jenny Foster (his father's sister) and the monument of Mr. and Mrs. E.L. Brown, longtime friends. On April 30, 1938, Ada Taft returned to Elmwood to unveil Taft's small bronze sculpture, "Memory," at the cemetery.[250] (It had been modeled after the 1923 William A. Foote Memorial.)

As his estate was settled up, newspapers were quick to report that Taft left a mere $10,000 to his family, but spent at least a quarter of a million dollars helping young sculptors, working on unsubsidized projects, and planning his dream museum.[251] Many had watched him dispense with his income, including his own brother-in-law Hamlin Garland, who talked about Taft's "kindly but unwarranted aid to struggling young artists":

> "[Taft] argues, however, that, as one is called upon to build great groups of outdoor sculpture, it is necessary to have a large studio and to maintain a force of assistants in order that certain results may be achieved within his lifetime. In this there is logic, but some of us still think that his humanitarian overhead charges are too great. … He lives very simply not far from his studio, and while he has earned a great deal of money, he has never used it for any personal luxury. It has all gone back into his art, into the extension of his studio plant, and in aid of young talent. In fact, some of us feel that too much of his energy has gone into plans for making life easier for those whose talent he recognizes. Some of his friends believe it would be better for his disciples if they were forced to struggle a little harder – and that to be a little less dependent upon their patron would be salutary."[252]

Taft's memorial and the cemetery's commemorative plaque

So where does Taft stand in the ranks of sculptors?

When Wayne Craven succeeded Taft as America's expert on sculpture and published *Sculpture in America* in 1968, he included only a brief mention of Taft, explaining that he "has fallen into virtual obscurity, except perhaps in the Chicago area, where his works are best known."[253] Is this really true?

Williams commented:

> *"Within the terms of his own tradition, and in relation to the work of his American contemporaries, Lorado Taft proved himself a skillful, intelligent, and gifted sculptor. Of flashing genius there is little evidence; of sensitivity, high integrity, and an understanding of the possibilities of his trade there is a great deal. It is possible, of course, to challenge the traditions and goals for which he strove, but the consistent and tasteful way in which he represented them still would be enviable. Taft was not a genius. He was a good sculptor."*[254]

Allen Weller succinctly summarized Taft's long and extensive art career in one paragraph:

> *"Taft presents an interesting case of an artist who during the greater part of his career considered himself and was generally considered to be in the mainstream of contemporary art in Chicago. He suddenly found himself unsympathetic to new artistic movements, while he also discovered that his work was being rejected by his younger contemporaries. Almost in spite of himself, he was influenced – at least briefly in the 1930s – by some of the new movements championed by those contemporaries. Indeed he was a bridge, though an unwilling one, between the full flower of the Beaux-Arts tradition of the 1893 World's Columbian Exposition and the new and very different art world of the 1930s."*[255]

Many of Taft's pieces continue to be treated with great respect, although his name is fading as a prominent sculptor, speaker, and author. No artist has stepped up to take his multifaceted place. How ironic that the phrase he used for his "Fountain of Time" – "Time stays, we go" – might apply to his work as well! The art world needs a spokesperson who will once again enthuse the general public with stories of past artists and spark them to the joys of creating a work of beauty from a slab of clay — someone who can once again instill an appreciation of how sculpture circles around and around, picking up new concepts but then returning to the time-honored designs of Greek, Roman, and European sculptors. Taft's small but loyal following bears the great responsibility for making sure that children of every generation are introduced to great sculpture and will learn to appreciate and treasure it.

ENDNOTES

The Earliest Years

1   Lorado Taft, "Why I have found life worth living," *The Christian Century*, June 7, 1923, p. 726
2   "Don Carlos Taft" in Amherst College Biographical Record: Class of 1852,
    http://www3.amherst.edu/~rjyanco94/genealogy/acbiorecord/1852.html
3   Ada Bartlett Taft, *Lorado Taft: Sculptor and Citizen* (published by Mary Taft Smith, Greensboro, N.C., 1946),
    p. 1. (Elmwood, Ill., is now the home to the Lorado Taft Museum, maintained by the Elmwood Historical
    Society at 302 North Magnolia. It includes a model of one of Taft's studio spaces and sculpting tools that
    students can hold and use on small pieces of stone, plus Taft's Phi Beta Kappa key, given to the museum by
    his daughter, Emily; letters Taft wrote and a plaster cast of a bust he completed – a gift from his family after
    his death; and a cabinet now used as a display case that was built by Taft's father around 1860 to house his
    own geological collection.)
4   Lewis W. Williams II, *Lorado Taft: American Sculptor and Art Missionary*, dissertation submitted to the faculty
    of the Division of the Humanities in candidacy for the degree of Doctor of Philosophy, Department of Art,
    the University of Chicago, March 1958, p. 2
5   Ada Bartlett Taft, p. 3
6   The house was located at Sixth and John streets. Williams dissertation, p. 5
7   Richard A. Coon and Nancy C. Coon, with assistance from Bill Knight, *Remembering a Favorite Son: The Story
    of Lorado Taft* (Elmwood Historical Society, Elmwood, Illinois, 2003), pp. 7-8
8   Ada Bartlett Taft, p. 77
9   Lorado Taft, "Why I have found life worth living," p. 725
10 "Lorado Taft … and the Utopian White City," *Iliniwek*, Sept.-Oct., 1972, Vol. 10, No. 4, p. 26, from Richard M.
    Phillips' archives, University of Illinois at Springfield Archives/Special Collections
11 Bulletin of the Krannert Art Museum, "Lorado Taft: A Retrospective Exhibition: January 16 to February 20,
    1983," Vol. VIII, Number 2 (University of Illinois, Urbana-Champaign, 1983), p. 2
12 "Establishing the sculpture program at the University of Illinois,"
    http://www.wpamurals.com/illsculpt.htm
13 Coon & Coon, p. 8
14 Williams dissertation, p. 15
15 Allen Stuart Weller, *Lorado in Paris: The Letters of Lorado Taft, 1880-1885* (Urbana and Chicago: University of
    Illinois Press, 1985). Weller's obituary is included in Appendix B.
16 From catalog from "Rodin: A Magnificent Obsession," exhibit sponsored by the Iris & B. Gerald Cantor
    Foundation, p. 3
17 Wikipedia, http://en.wikipedia.org/wiki/Lorado_Taft
18 Bulletin of the Krannert Art Museum, p. 2
19 Lorado Taft letter, August 6, 1880, quoted in Williams dissertation, p. 23
20 Lorado Taft, "The McAll Mission", MS, ca. 1887. Reprinted in slightly varied form as: "The McAll Mission,"
    Chicago Interocean, September 18, 1887, quoted in Williams dissertation, p. 22
21 Williams dissertation, p. 41
22 Lorado Taft letter dated August 22, 1884, quoted in Williams dissertation, p. 44
23 James Krohe, Jr., "Reading: Exterior Decoration," in *Chicago Reader*, August 12, 1988
24 Williams dissertation, p. 47
25 Williams dissertation, p. 50
26 Ada Bartlett Taft, p. 18
27 Williams dissertation, p. 71
28 Coon & Coon, pp. 9-10

Teaching and Lecturing

29 Timothy J. Garvey, *Public Sculptor: Lorado Taft and the Beautification of Chicago* (Urbana and Chicago:
    University of Chicago Press, 1988), p. 46
30 Taft, "Why I have found life worth living," pp. 725-726
31 Williams dissertation, p. 56

32   University of Chicago faculty: Lorado Taft, http://www.lib.uchicago.edu/e/spcl/centcat/fac/facch19_01.html

33   Ada Bartlett Taft, p. 26

34   Lorado Taft letter, May 10, 1899, cited in Williams dissertation, p. 75

35   Garvey, p. 47

36   Williams dissertation, p. 79

37   Coon & Coon, p. 13

38   Charles Francis Browne, "Lorado Taft: Sculptor," *World Today*, XIV (February, 1908), p. 193, cited in Williams dissertation, p. 83

39   Williams dissertation, p. 83

40   *The Art Institute of Chicago: the essential guide*, selected by James N. Wood and Teri J. Edelstein: with entries compiled and written by Sally Ruth May (Chicago: The Art Institute of Chicago, 1993)

41   Taft, Lorado, *American Sculpture* (New York: The Macmillan Company, 1925)

42   Lorado Taft entry, Wikipedia, http://en.wikipedia.org/wiki/Lorado_Taft

43   Ada Bartlett Taft, p. 25

44   Bulletin of the Krannert Art Museum, p. 5

45   Lorado Taft entry, http://www.answers.com/topic/lorado-taft

46   Eleanor Jewett, "Lorado Taft to Sculpture New Memorial," *Chicago Sunday Tribune*, August 9, 1936

47   Ada Bartlett Taft, p. 75

48   Lorado Taft, *Modern Tendencies in Sculpture (The Scammon Lectures for 1917)* (Chicago: University of Chicago Press, 1921)

49   Lorado Taft entry, Wikipedia, http://en.wikipedia.org/wiki/Lorado_Taft

50   Bulletin of the Krannert Art Museum, p. 5. Also cited in Williams dissertation, p. 80

51   American Expeditionary Forces University, Catalogue Bulletin: Part I (Published by Order of Col. Reeves, May 1919), cited in Williams dissertation, p. 106

52   Krannert Art Museum Bulletin, p. 5

53   Krannert Art Museum Bulletin, p. 5

54   Williams dissertation, p. 116

55   Henry Regnery, *The Cliff Dwellers* (Evanston: Chicago Historical Bookworks, 1990) pp. 3-4

56   Williams dissertation, p. 69

57   Regnery, p.7

58   Regnery, p.11

59   Regnery, p.13

60   Harold Henderson, "Above It All," *Chicago Reader*, October 27, 1994

61   Regnery, p. 39

62   Cliff Dwellers Club website: http://www.cliff-chicago.org

Portraiture

63   Trygve A. Rovelstad, "Impressions of Lorado Taft," *Papers in Illinois History*, (Springfield, Illinois: The Illinois State Historical Society, 1938), p. 23

64   Williams dissertation, p. 52

65   Williams dissertation, p. 51

66   Williams dissertation, p. 281

67   Tim Obermiller, "A matter of time," *University of Chicago Magazine*, February 1991, p. 24

68   Garvey, p. 59, quoting Taft, "Dreams and Death Masks," *Chicago Record*, June 6, 1899, p. 4

69   Krannert Art Museum Bulletin, p. 3

70   Robert H. Moulton, "Lorado Taft and his work as a sculptor," *The American Review of Reviews*, June 1912, p. 721

71   Timothy J. Garvey, "Conferring Status: Lorado Taft's Portraits of an Artistic Community," *Illinois Historical Journal*, Vol. 78: Fall 1985, pp. 162-178

Frances Willard

72   Frances Willard, *A Classic Town: The Story of Evanston by "An Old Timer,"* Women's Temperance Publication Association, Chicago, 1892, p. 362 and on inset between pp. 184 and 185

73   The Rest Cottage, Willard's Evanston home, is now both an Evanston Landmark and a National Historic Landmark and is managed by the Frances Willard Historical Association. It is open for guided tours: see its website, www.franceswillardhouse.org.

74   Yahoo quotations, http://education.yahoo.com/reference/quotations/quote/74831

75   "Taft's Bust of Miss Willard to be presented to Northwestern University to-day by John C. Shaffer," *Chicago Times-Herald*, June 13, 1898

76   Copy of address by Frank P. Crandon, June 13, 1898, from Northwestern University Archives

77   The Hall of Fame for Great Americans – Face-to-Face Online Tour, http://www.bcc.cuny.edu/HallofFame

78   Sarah F. Ward, *Ella A. Boole: Dauntless Leader*, Signal Press, Evanston, Illinois, 2007, pp. 17-18

79   "Taft's Bust of Miss Willard to be presented to Northwestern University to-day by John C. Shaffer," *Chicago Times-Herald*, June 13, 1898

Civil War Monuments

80   Rovelstad, p. 23

81   3rd Michigan Infantry (1889) (in the Peach Orchard); 4th Michigan Infantry (1889) (in the Wheatfield at DeTrobriand Avenue); 5th Michigan Infantry (1889) (east of the Loop at Sickles Avenue); and Custer's Michigan Cavalry Brigade (1889) (in East Cavalry Field on Custer Avenue)

82   In addition, he designed the figures for a Soldiers and Sailors Monument (1891) in Mt. Carroll, Ill., and sculpted bronze statues for the Civil War Soldiers and Sailors Monument (1891) at Philipse Manor Hall in Yonkers, N.Y.; the Soldiers and Sailor Monument (1892) in Winchester, Ind.; and the Soldier's Monument (1916) in Oregon, Ill.

83   Michael W. Panhorst, "Outdoor Sculpture in Jackson, Michigan," http://www.ellasharp.org/our-outdoor-sculpture.html

Grave Memorials

84   Williams dissertation, pp. 219-220

85   A second casting, in more weathered condition, sits in the center courtyard of the Midway Studios.

86   Michael W. Panhorst on William A. Foote Memorial, http://www.ellasharp.org/pages/SOS4.html

Columbian Exposition

87   Krannert Art Museum Bulletin, p. 3

88   "Lorado Taft … and the Utopian White City," p. 27

89   Taft obituary, "Lorado Taft Dies: Leading Sculptor," *The New York Times*, October 31, 1936, p. 19.

90   Obermiller, p. 24

91   "Lorado Taft … and the Utopian White City," p. 27

92   Zulime Taft Garland, "Recollections of Lorado Taft," MS, ca. 1937. Typescript in Taft Collection, cited by Williams dissertation, p. 66. Although Zulime lists only these six women, a list of "White Rabbits" from the Lorado Taft entry in the "American Masters" catalog, Brookgreen Gardens, Murrells Inlet, S.C., 1996, p. 55, includes Helen Farnsworth Mears, Margaret Gerow, Mary Lawrence (Tonetti) and Evalyn Longman. Williams lists Ella Rankin Copp as one of the White Rabbits, and also a man, Leonard Crunelle, who remained with Taft for many years, first as assistant and later as a sculptor in his own right. (Williams dissertation, p. 66). Also, see entry on White Rabbits in Wikipedia, http://en.wikipedia.org/wiki/White_Rabbits.

93   Williams dissertation, p. 66

94   Janet Scudder, *Modeling My Life* (New York: Harcourt Brace, 1925), pp. 52-60, quoted in Williams dissertation, pp. 65-66

95   Williams dissertation, p. 84

Fountains

96   Garvey, p. 40

97   Garvey, p. 56, quoting Patricia Erens, *Masterpieces: Famous Chicagoans and Their Paintings* (Chicago: Chicago Review Press, 1979); and "The Great Grey City," *Apollo: The Magazine of the Arts*, 84 (September 1966), pp. 172-77

98   Urbana and Chicago: University of Illinois Press, 1988

99   Garvey, p. 57

100   Garvey, p. 37, quoting from the "Address of Lorado Taft," Dedication of the Ferguson Fountain of the Great Lakes, p. 26

101   Garvey, p. 60, quoting from the "Address of Lorado Taft," Dedication of the Ferguson Fountain of the Great Lakes, p. 26

102   Address by Lorado Taft, Exercises at the dedication of the Ferguson Fountain of the Great Lakes, Chicago, September 9, 1913, pp. 26, 28

103   Garvey, p. 12

104   Garvey, p. 12

105   Garvey, p. 11, quoting Shaler Mathews, "Uncommercial Chicago," *World To-Day*, 9 (September 1905), p. 990

106   Garvey, p. 16

107   Garvey. p. 15

108   Garvey. p. 15

109   Garvey, p. 18, quoting from "Fountain Soon to Run," *Chicago Daily News*, May 10, 1913, p. 6

110   Allen Weller, "Lorado Taft, the Ferguson Fund, and the Advent of Modernism," in *The Old Guard and the Avant-Garde: Modernism in Chicago, 1910-1940*, Sue Ann Prince, ed. (Chicago: University of Chicago Press, 1990), p. 41

111   Garvey, p. 3

112   Garvey, p. 151, quoting Harriet Monroe, "Lake Monument Triumph in Art," *Chicago Tribune*, September 14, 1913, II, p. 5

113   Garvey, p. 155, quoting *Chicago Daily News*: "The Spirit of the Great Lakes ready, and Lake Michigan in a Spirited Mood Coincidentally," September 9, 1913, p. 3

114   Garvey, p. 158, referring to the proceedings of the City Council from March 31, 1913

115   Photo copyright by Antonio Vernon, June 23, 2007, published in Wikipedia, http://en.wikipedia.org/wiki/File:20070621_Fountain_of_the_Great_Lakes_(rear).jpg

116   James Krohe, Jr., quoting James L. Riedy, *Chicago Sculpture* (Chicago: University of Chicago Press, 1981)

117   Williams dissertation, p. 216

118   Bill Kemp, Archivist/Librarian, McLean County Museum of History, "'Trotter Fountain' work of Lorado Taft," www.Pantagraph.com, February 9, 2008

119   Moulton, p. 725

120   Moulton, p. 724

121   James Loewen, "The Sociology of Selected Monuments in Washington, DC, or Stories Behind the Stories," in *Footnotes* (newsletter of the American Sociological Association), Vol. 28, No. 4, April 2000, http://www.asanet.org/footnotes/apr00/stones.html

122   "Denver's Historic Fountains," Denver Parks and Recreation website, http://198.202.202.66/Parks/template 21961.asp

Abraham Lincoln, Stephen Douglas, and other historical figures

123   Champaign County. Urbana. Lincoln, in *National Register News*, October 2004

124   Siegfried R. Weng obituary, *Evansville Courier & Press*, February 21, 2008. From collection of newspaper clippings and other Taft-related materials from Miss Elizabeth Bensen

125   Williams dissertation, p. 201

126   Lorado Taft, "Draft for Dedication Talk," MS, June, 1927, cited in Williams dissertation, p. 119. Williams went on to point out that Taft used for Lincoln's face "the invaluable Volk mask." In 1860 sculptor Leonard Volk made a life mask of Lincoln's face and Lincoln's hands out of plaster. In 1885-1886, a fund drive was begun to purchase these plaster pieces for the National Museum (now the Smithsonian). A copy in plaster sold for $50, and bronze copies cost subscribers $85. One of the bronze copies is on display at Chicago's Glessner House Museum. (Glessner House Museum website, http://glessnerhouse.org/Lincoln.html)

127   Garvey, p. 91, quoting "Ready for the Dedication," *Indianapolis Journal*, May 27, 1887, p. 5

128   Garvey, p. 91, quoting Taft in Garland, *Roadside Meetings* (New York: Macmillan Co., 1930), p. 264

129   Fort Leavenworth History, "What is the history of the Grant statue on post?," http://usacac.army.mil/CAC/csi/faqs.asp

130 Leavenworth County Monuments and Memorials,
http:///www.rmtci.com/CWMM_KS/Leavenworth-county.html
131 HistoryLink.org Essay 8666, "Alaska-Yukon-Pacific Exposition in Seattle celebrates Pullman Day, Flag Day, and Sons and Daughters of the American Revolution Day on June 14, 1909,"
http://www.historylink.org/index.cfm?DisplayPage=output.cfm&file_id=8666
132 Ada Bartlett Taft, p. 48
133 "The Annie Louise Keller Memorial," undated. From collection of newspaper clippings and other Taft-related materials from Miss Elizabeth Bensen

Low-relief Panels
134 Williams dissertation, p. 213
135 Williams lists other portraits in his dissertation, but their existences have not been confirmed: Everette Buckingham (1926), in the rotunda of the Live Stock Exchange Building in Omaha, Nebraska; and Delta Tau Delta Memorial (1921), at the DTD Fraternity Building at the University of Illinois.
136 Mark Skertic, "Treasure hunt: Officials work to find the city's lost art," *Chicago Sun-Times*, October 30, 1998, Metro section, p. 9
137 "Historic City Hall Plaque to be rededicated," CBSChicago.com, November 4, 2010, 2:14 pm

Medals
138 Photo was taken in 1901 by Fred A. Hetherington of Indianapolis, from the booklet that accompanied each medal, "A MEDAL struck in celebration of the sixty-sixth anniversary of the birth of James Whitcomb Riley, and done in bronze by Lorado Taft on the commission of one hundred of the poet's admiring fellow townsmen," (Indianapolis: The Hollenbeck Press).
139 The Lilly Library in Bloomington, Indiana, owns one of these pieces; the Art Institute of Chicago owns two; the Peoria Art Museum owns one; and the Eagles Nest Art Collection owns one. They also occasionally appear on eBay; one in excellent, uncirculated condition sold in July 2012 for $389.
140 "Lorado Taft's Peace Medal," *Survey Graphic Magazine*, July 1938, (Vol. XXVII, January 1938-December 1938, p. 404). The images were originally obtained from the Lorado Taft Papers, Record Series 26/20/16, University of Illinois Archives.
141 James Michna, "Lorado Taft Reveals Youth's Attitude of War in New Medallion," *Daily Maroon*, January 30, 1935. From collection of newspaper clippings and other Taft-related materials from Miss Elizabeth Bensen
142 Williams dissertation, p. 142, citing Lorado Taft, letters to Medallic Arts Company, January 30; February 2 and February 21, 1935

Midway Studios
143 Williams dissertation, p. 52
144 Williams dissertation, p. 70
145 Williams dissertation, p. 72
146 Ada Bartlett Taft, p. 22
147 James Krohe, Jr., p. 2
148 Garvey, p. 53, quoting from a Taft letter to his family dated October 17, 1887, Box 6, Taft Papers, University of Illinois
149 Coon & Coon, p. 11
150 Ada Bartlett Taft, p. 28
151 Coon & Coon, p. 11
152 "Lorado Taft's Midway Studios," Chicago Landmarks website,
http://egov.cityofchicago.org/Landmarks/T/TaftMidway.html
153 Krannert Art Museum Bulletin, p. 5
154 Fred Torrey obituary, *Des Moines Register*, July 10, 1967, p. 9
155 J.V. Nash, "He Carves Mysticism Into Stone: Lorado Taft, Apostle of the Modern Renaissance," *The Dearborn Independent*, September 19, 1925. From collection of newspaper clippings and other Taft-related materials from Miss Elizabeth Bensen
156 "Freeman and Cora Schoolcraft: A Tribute," published in conjunction with a 2000 exhibition at the Morris Museum of Art, Augusta, GA, pp. 7-8

157   Ada Bartlett Taft, p. 32

The Gates of Paradise
158   Williams dissertation, pp. 128-130

Dream Museum & Peep Shows
159   Ada Bartlett Taft, p. 76
160   Lorado Taft, "Chicago's Historic Museum of Architecture and Sculpture: A World's Fair Suggestion by Lorado Taft." 4-page pamphlet, no publisher credit or date
161   Lorado Taft's Dream Museum, from *Glendale News-Press*, October 4, 1994, http://english.glendale.cc.ca.us/taft.html
162   "Lorado Taft work on display," *Evansville Courier*, October 23, 1938, Section D, p. 1
163   Krannert Art Museum Bulletin, p. 6
164   Donald Mokelke, Curator of Education, "The Lorado Z. Taft 'Peep Show' Dioramas depicting early sculptors as exhibited in the Kenosha Public Museum," 1971, unnumbered p. 3
165   Ada Bartlett Taft, p. 31
166   Email correspondence to Young from Jennifer White, University of Illinois, Urbana-Champaign, July 28, 2005

Eagle's Nest Colony
167   Williams dissertation, p. 73
168   June Sawyers, "The Taft legacy: great art crafted from big dreams," in *Chicago Tribune*, January 18, 1987
169   Williams dissertation, pp. 102-103
170   Garvey, p. 108, referring to Harriet Monroe, "Eagle's Nest Camp: A Colony of Artists and Writers," *House Beautiful*, 16 (August 1904), pp. 5-10
171   "Eagle's Nest Art Colony," Lorado Taft Field Campus website, http://www.niu.edu/taft/eagles.htm
172   Jan Stilson, *Art and Beauty in the Heartland* (Bloomington, Indiana: AuthorHouse, 2006), ISBN 9781425938611 (paperback)
173   Catalog of the Eagle's Nest Art Colony Collection, Oregon, Illinois, published by the Arts Alliance of Ogle County, 1982. Website catalog: http://www.oregon.lib.il.us/eagles-nest-art-gallery.html
174   From "The Story of the Four Little Children Who Went Round the World," published in *A Book of Nonsense by Edward Lear with all the original pictures and verses* (Boston: Roberts Brothers, 1894), transcribed in 2004 by The Project Gutenberg eBook, Nonsense Books, by Edward Lear, http://www.gutenberg.org/files/13650/13650-h/13650-h.htm#children

Black Hawk and other Native Americans
175   Krannert Art Museum Bulletin, p. 4
176   Rovelstad, p. 28
177   J. V. Nash, no page number
178   Williams dissertation, pp. 88-90
179   Vinde Wells, *Ogle County News*, June 12, 2008
180   Harry Spell is a retired professor from Bradley University with his own casting company, Art Casting of Illinois. Spell did not charge for his labor but only for materials.
181   Originally sited in front of the Paducah Post Office, it was moved after the Ohio Valley Flood of June 1937 and now sits on the median strip at 19th and Jefferson streets.
182   *American Experience: Mount Rushmore*, www.pbs.org/wgbh/amex/rushmore/peopleevents/p_robinson.html

Plan for Chicago's Midway Plaisance
183   Lorado Taft, quoted in "Midway To Be Dream In Marble," *Chicago Interocean*, May 22, 1910, cited in Williams dissertation, p. 94
184   "For these bridges I.K. Pond made distinguished drawings." Ada Bartlett Taft, p. 34

185 "Taft did not plan to execute all of these [statues] himself, and envisioned a sort of vast cooperative effort – not unlike the decoration of the Columbian Exposition – which could furnish employment to many artists. A favorite game in the Midway Studios was composing lists of individuals to be included." Williams dissertation, p. 95

186 Garvey, p. 149, quoting "Taft Begins Statue," *Chicago Daily News*, February 15, 1913, p. 5

187 Ada Bartlett Taft, pp. 34-35

188 Rovelstad, p. 32

189 Hamlin Garland, "A Mid-Western Sculptor: The Art of Lorado Taft," *The Mentor*, October 1923, Serial No. 248. p. 24

190 Garvey, p. 161, quoting Roswell Field, "Why Not Localize That Midway Art?" *Chicago Examiner*, May 8, 1910

191 Jeff Huebner, "Can This Patient Be Saved?", *Chicago Reader*, December 6, 2002, Vol. 32, No. 10, p. 30

192 Ada Bartlett Taft, pp. 38, 39

193 Obermiller, p. 26, citing Allen Weller

194 John Drury, "Lorado at 76; Devotes the Entire Day to His Art," April 28, 1936. From collection of newspaper clippings and other Taft-related materials from Miss Elizabeth Bensen

195 "American Masters" catalog, p. 55

196 Ada Bartlett Taft, p. 35

Fountain of Time

197 Garvey, p. 145, quoting Taft to Trustees of the Art Institute, n.d., laid on "Minutes of the Trustees of the Art Institute," typescript, January 30, 1913 [p. 1], copy in Box 12, Taft Papers, University of Illinois

198 H.A. Dobson, *Collected Poems* (London: Kegan Paul, Trench, Trübner & Co. Ltd., 1905)

199 Garvey, p. 146, quoting "Fountain of Time Modeling Given to Lorado Taft," *Chicago Inter Ocean*, February 1, 1913, p. 3

200 Obermiller, p. 26

201 "Time" Marches On," from "The Urban Observer" blog posted by Lee Bey on June 11, 2007, http://leebey.com/blog1/2007/06

202 Obermiller, p. 26, quoting Taft

203 Obermiller, p. 26, quoting Taft

204 Martha Blastow, "Time Tested," from *Concrete Products Magazine*, December 1, 2002, http://concreteproducts.com/mag/concrete_time_tested

205 James L. Riedy, *Chicago Sculpture* (University of Illinois Press, 1981), p. 50

206 'Detailed Description of the Fountain of Time," Lorado Taft Papers, Ryerson Library, Art Institute of Chicago, quoted in Riedy, p. 49

207 Rovelstad, p. 32

208 Obermiller, p. 22

209 Obermiller, p. 22, citing "More Pet Atrocities, *Chicago Tribune*, January 6, 1926

210 Garvey, p. 173, quoting "More Pet Atrocities"

211 "Alan Artner chooses Chicago's best public sculpture," *Chicago Tribune*, May 1, 2008

212 Obermiller, p. 20, citing Robert Jones

213 Bill Grainger, "Unfortunately for sculptor Taft, indifference and austerity are formidable foes of posterity," *Chicago Tribune*, June 18, 1989

214 Huebner, pp. 30-31

215 Huebner, p. 32

216 Huebner, p. 32

217 Huebner is quoting Robert Jones, a former deputy architect with the Park District who oversaw projects at the Lincoln Park Zoo and Soldier Field, who was hired to oversee the Art Institute's design and construction staff. Jones was heavily involved in the conservation effort.

218 Andrew Herrmann, "Money flows to rehab Fountain of Time pool," *Chicago Sun-Times,* June 8, 2005, p. 8

The Elmwood "Pioneers"

219 Coon & Coon, pp. 16-17

220 Krannert Art Museum Bulletin, p. 6. A bronzed plaster version of "The Pioneers" is located at the south entrance to the University Library in Urbana, Ill.
221 Coon & Coon, pp. 17-18

Alma Mater
222 Krannert Art Museum Bulletin, p. 6
223 Krannert Art Museum Bulletin, p. 6
224 Krannert Art Museum Bulletin, p. 6
225 Krannert Art Museum Bulletin, p. 2
226 Williams dissertation, p. 219
227 http://www.library.illinois.edu/archives/ead/ua/2620016/2620016f.html

Chicago's Century of Progress
228 Weller, p. 46
229 Obermiller, p. 26
230 Weller, p. 55

Louisiana's State Capitol
231 Vincent F. Kubly, *The Louisiana Capitol: Its Art and Architecture* (Gretna: Pelican Publishing Company, 1995).
232 Kubly, pp. 35-37, includes quotes from "New Capitol Represents Efforts to Tell History in Enduring Materials," *Baton Rouge State Times*, May 16, 1932
233 Williams dissertation, pp. 133-134, citing Lorado Taft letters, February 1, 1932
234 Williams dissertation, pp. 200-201

Nearing the end
235 Lorado Taft's Dream Museum, from *Glendale News-Press*, Oct. 4, 1994, http://english.glendale.cc.ca.us/taft.html
236 "Lorado Taft Is Dead; World-Famous Sculptor," *Chicago Daily News*, October 30, 1936, p. 1. From collection of newspaper clippings and other Taft-related materials from Miss Elizabeth Bensen
237 "Associates of Lorado Taft Carry on Unfinished Work," undated. From collection of newspaper clippings and other Taft-related materials from Miss Elizabeth Bensen
238 Riedy, p. 214
239 Harry Barnard, *This Great Triumvirate of Patriots* (Chicago: Follett Publishing Company, 1971)

Krannert Art Museum Exhibition
240 List provided as of August 25, 2009, indicates 176 pieces in the collection.
241 Krannert Art Museum Bulletin, p. 24

The Blind
242 Rovelstad, pp. 26, 27
243 Catalog from the dedication of "The Blind," Krannert Art Museum, University of Illinois at Urbana Champaign, copy written by Allen Weller, 1988, pp. 7-9
244 "The Blind" catalog, pp. 13-15

Mysteries solved...
245 Glory-June Greiff, *Remembrance, Faith and Fancy: Outdoor Public Sculpture in Indiana* (Indianapolis: Indiana Historical Society, 2005), ISBN: 0871951800
246 Crown Hill Cemetery "Notable Persons" website, http://crownhill.org/cemetery/persons.html

Pieces we can't see...
247 Marilou McCarthy, "They Were There," *Chicago Daily Tribune*, July 19, 1961, p. A2

And new discoveries...
248 Newspaper credit line was cut off of article included with eBay purchase.

Exciting plans for the future.
249 "Katharine Sharp goes digital," June 28, 2011,
    http://www.lis.illinois.edu/articles/2011/06/katharine-sharp-goes-digital

Taft's death
250 Coon & Coon, pp. 20-21
251 "Faily Tells of Taft's Gifts to Students," undated. From collection of newspaper clippings and other Taft-related materials from Miss Elizabeth Bensen
252 Garland, p. 21-22

So where does Taft stand in the ranks of sculptors?
253 Wayne Craven, *Sculpture in America*. New and rev. ed. (Newark: University of Delaware Press; New York: Cornwall, 1984), p. 494
254 Williams dissertation, p. 224
255 Weller, p. 57

Appendix A
256 *Chicago Theological Seminary Register*, XXVII (January 1937) pp. 5-8

Appendix B
257 *Champaign-Urbana News-Gazette*, Tuesday, November 18, 1997

Appendix C
258 *Beloit Daily News*, Tuesday, August 7, 1990

Appendix D
259 List is updated from Weller, pp. 226-276

Photo Credits

Frontis   Lorado Taft seated by model for *Fountain of Time*: Courtesy of the University of Illinois Archives, ID# 0006092, ca. 1917-1918, found in RS: 26/20/16, Box 31, #105. Copyright Jane Reece

viii   "Spirit of Art": Courtesy of the Krannert Art Museum, University of Illinois, Urbana-Champaign, Ill. Lent to Krannert by Midway Studios, The University of Chicago

1   Taft birthplace: from the Illinois Artists Project, Lynn Allyn Young personal collection

2   Taft House, original view: Courtesy of the University of Illinois Archives, ID# 0001850, April 8, 1940, found in RS: 39/2/20, Box BUI Taft House, Folder BUI Taft House 1940-1973. Copyright University of Illinois

2   Lorado Taft Grandparents Gazette Map, ca. May 1874. Courtesy of the University of Illinois Archives, found in RS 26/20/16, Box 2, Folder: Grandparents Gazette, originals, 1874-75

3   Art Gallery: M. Phillips' personal photographic collection, University of Illinois at Springfield Archives/Special Collections

4   Lorado Taft in Beaux Arts class, Paris: Courtesy of the University of Illinois Archives, ID# 0006090, ca. 1881-1885, found in RS: 26/20/16, Box 31, #131. The holder of this copyright is unknown.

5   Modeling Class at Art Institute: Courtesy of the University of Illinois Archives, ID# 0002716, ca. 1896, found in RS 26/20/16, Box 26, Folder Art Institute Classes. The holder of this copyright is unknown.

6   "Solitude of the Soul": from uncredited vintage postcard

7   "Silence of the Soul": Photograph by Lynn Allyn Young. Courtesy of the Art Institute of Chicago, Chicago, Ill.

8   Lorado Taft in studio: Courtesy of the University of Illinois Archives, ID#0001214, found in RS: 26/20/16, ca. 1910s, found in RS: 26/20/16, Box 25, Folder Photographs of the Midway Studios. The holder of this copyright is unknown.

8   "Knowledge" and "Despair": Photograph by Lynn Allyn Young. Courtesy of the Rockford Art Museum, Rockford, Ill.

9   Travel brochure: Collection of Miss Betty Benson

10   Lorado Taft and members of the Cliff Dwellers Club: Courtesy of the Cliff Dwellers Club/Ragdale Foundation

11   Lorado Taft at Cliff Dwellers table: Courtesy of the Newberry Library, Chicago. Call #MMS Cliff, 3a 24-10-11.

12   Henry Hardin Cherry: Photograph by Lynn Allyn Young. Courtesy of Western Kentucky University, Bowling Green, Ky.

13   Charles Hackley Memorial: Photograph by Lynn Allyn Young. Courtesy of City of Muskegon, Mich.

13   Thomas D. Gilbert: Photograph by Lynn Allyn Young. Courtesy of City of Grand Rapids, Mich.

13   Charles Page Memorial: Photograph by Lynn Allyn Young. Courtesy of City of Sand Springs, Okla.

17   Busts:

Ella Pomeroy Belden: Photograph by Lynn Allyn Young. Courtesy of the Lorado Taft Museum, Elmwood, Ill.

Prof. George Washington Northrup: Photograph by Lynn Allyn Young. Courtesy of the University of Chicago, Chicago, Ill.

Pres. Edward Dwight Eaton: Photograph by Lynn Allyn Young. Courtesy of Beloit College, Beloit, Wisc.

Mrs. Wallace Heckman: Photograph by Lynn Allyn Young. Courtesy of The Oregon Illinois Public Library's Eagles' Nest Art Colony Collection

Ozora Stearns Davis and Franklin Woodbury Fisk: Photograph by Lynn Allyn Young. Courtesy of Chicago Theological Seminary

Pres. George F. Magoun: Photograph by Lynn Allyn Young. Courtesy of Grinnell College, Grinnell, Iowa

Silas B. Cobb: Photograph by Lynn Allyn Young. Courtesy of the University of Chicago, Chicago, Ill.

John Crerar: Photograph by Lynn Allyn Young. Courtesy of the John Crerar Library, University of Chicago Library, Chicago, Ill.

18   Frances Willard bust: Photograph by Lynn Allyn Young. Courtesy of the Northwestern University archives, Evanston, Ill.

18   Frances Willard medallion: Photograph by Lynn Allyn Young. Courtesy of Rest Cottage, Evanston, Ill.

18   Taft with Frances Willard bust: Photo by John D. Jones, *Chicago Tribune*, August 20, 1929, courtesy of the Northwestern University archives, Evanston, Ill.

19   Frances Willard plaque: Photograph by Dale Crabtree. Courtesy of Indiana State Capitol, Indianapolis, Ind.

19   Frances Willard bust: Photograph by Lynn Allyn Young. Courtesy of WCTU Library, Evanston, Ill.

19   Hall of Fame for Great Americans: Photograph by Lynn Allyn Young. Courtesy of Bronx Community College, Bronx, N.Y.

20   Soldier's Monument: Photograph by Lynn Allyn Young. Courtesy of City of Oregon, Ill.

20   War Monument: Photograph by Lynn Allyn Young. Courtesy of City of Mt. Carroll, Ill.

20   War Memorial and frieze: Photographs by Lynn Allyn Young. Courtesy of City of Winchester, Ind.

21   Custer's Monument: Photograph by Lynn Allyn Young. Courtesy of Gettysburg National Military Park, Gettysburg, Penn.

21   Admiral Porter: Photograph by Lynn Allyn Young. Courtesy of Vicksburg National Military Park, Vicksburg, Miss.

21   Monuments to 5th, 4th, and 3rd Michigan Infantry: Photographs by Lynn Allyn Young. Courtesy of Gettysburg National Military Park, Gettysburg, Penn.

22   "Victory" Monument: Photograph by Lynn Allyn Young. Courtesy of City of Danville, Ill.

22   Sketch Model for Soldier's Memorial, Omaha, Nebraska: Courtesy of the University of Illinois Archives, ID# 0006085, ca. 1925, found in RS: 26/20/16, Box 30, #72. The holder of this copyright is unknown.

22   Soldier's Monument, Albany, New York: Courtesy of the University of Illinois Archives, ID# 0006087, ca. 1900s, found in RS: 26/20/16, Box 30, #101. The holder of this copyright is unknown.

23   "Defense of the Flag" Monument: Photograph by Lynn Allyn Young. Courtesy of City of Jackson, Mich.

23   "Defense of the Flag" Monument: Photograph by Lynn Allyn Young. Courtesy of Marion National Cemetery, U.S. Department of Veterans Affairs

23   "Defense of the Flag" Monument: Photograph by Lynn Allyn Young. Courtesy of Chickamauga National Military Park, Chickamauga, Ga.

24   "Eternal Silence" Memorial: Photograph by Lynn Allyn Young. Courtesy of Graceland Cemetery, Chicago, Ill.

25   "Recording Angel" Memorial: Photograph by Lynn Allyn Young. Courtesy of Forest Mound Cemetery, Waupun, Wisc.

25   Foote Memorial: Photograph by Lynn Allyn Young. Courtesy of Woodland Cemetery, Jackson, Mich.

25   "The Crusader" Memorial: Photograph by Lynn Allyn Young. Courtesy of Graceland Cemetery, Chicago, Ill.

26   Horticulture Building photo: Photograph by William H. Jackson, published 1895. Print purchased from Period Paper, www.stores.ebay.com/PeriodPaper.

27   "Awakening of the Flowers" Figure Group: Courtesy of the University of Illinois Archives, ID# 0006083, ca. 1893, found in RS: 26/20/16, Box 30, #5. The holder of this copyright is unknown.

27   "Sleep of the Flowers," "Pomona" and "Flora": *Iliniwek*, Vol. 10, No. 4, September October 1972, from Richard M. Phillips' personal photographic collection, University of Illinois at Springfield Archives/Special Collections

28   Horticulture Building studio photo: *Iliniwek*, Vol. 10, No. 4, September October 1972, from Richard M. Phillips' personal photographic collection, University of Illinois at Springfield Archives/Special Collections

29   "Idyll" and "Pastoral": Photographs by Lynn Allyn Young. Courtesy of the Garfield Park Conservatory, Chicago, Ill.

29   Fernery: from uncredited vintage postcard

31   Lafayette Fountain: Photograph by Lynn Allyn Young. Courtesy of Tippecanoe County, Lafayette, Ind.

32   Ferguson Fountain, DN-0061048, *Chicago Daily News* negatives collection, Chicago History Museum

32   Hidden Ferguson plaque: Photograph by Antonio Vernon, 21 June 2007, GFDL granted by photographer. From Wikimedia Commons, the free media repository

33   Ferguson Fountain: Photograph by Lynn Allyn Young. Courtesy of Art Institute of Chicago, Chicago, Ill.

34   Grinnell College coeds photo: Uncredited, from collection of Miss Betty Benson

35   Trotter Fountain and detail: Photographs by Lynn Allyn Young. Courtesy of City of Bloomington, Ind.

36   Columbus Fountain: Photograph by Lynn Allyn Young. Courtesy of City of Washington, D.C.

37   Thatcher Fountain and details: Photographs by Lynn Allyn Young. Courtesy of City of Denver, Colo.

38   "Fish Boys" Fountain: Photograph by Lynn Allyn Young. Courtesy of City of Oregon, Ill.

38   Taft with Fish Boy: Wikimedia Commons, from *Chicago Daily News*, 15 February 1913

39   Douglas plaques: Photographs by Lynn Allyn Young. Courtesy of Mandel Hall, University of Chicago, Chicago, Ill., and City of Brandon, Vt.

40   Taft with Lincoln statue: DN-0080734, *Chicago Daily News* negatives collection, Chicago History Museum

40   Lincoln statue: Photograph by Lynn Allyn Young. Courtesy of Lincoln's Tomb, Springfield, Ill.

40   "Young Lincoln" statue: Photograph by Lynn Allyn Young. Courtesy of City of Urbana, Ill.

41   Schulyer Colfax statue and low-relief panel: Photographs by Lynn Allyn Young. Courtesy of City of Indianapolis, Ind.

42   Ulysses S. Grant statue and Grant low-relief panel: Photographs by Lynn Allyn Young. Courtesy of Fort Leavenworth, U.S. Army, Leavenworth, Kans.

43   Washington statue: Photograph by Joe Mabel, 22 November 2009, GFDL granted by photographer. From Wikimedia Commons, the free media repository

43   Washington statue being hoisted: Wikimedia Commons, from Alaska-Yukon-Pacific Exposition Collection, Item Number: AYP143, University of Washington Libraries Digital Collections

43   Washington statue dedication: from Alaska-Yukon-Pacific Exposition Postcard Collection, Item Number: AYP969, University of Washington Libraries Digital Collections

44   Annie Louise Keller Memorial: Photograph by Lynn Allyn Young. Courtesy of City of White Hall, Ill.

45   Bobs Roberts: Photograph by Lynn Allyn Young. Courtesy of Comer Children's Hospital, Chicago, Ill.

45   Katharine Sharp plaque: Photograph by Daryl Quitalig, courtesy of University of Illinois Library

46   Iroquois Theater panel in boiler room: From *Chicago Sun-Times*, August 10, 1967, photo by Larry Nocerino. Lynn Allyn Young personal collection.

46   Iroquois Theater plaque: Photograph by Lynn Allyn Young. Courtesy of City Hall, Chicago, Ill.

47   Dolliver plaque: Photograph by Lynn Allyn Young. Courtesy of Dolliver State Park, State of Iowa

48   Peace Medal: From Douglas, Emily Taft, "Lorado Taft's Peace Medal," *Survey Graphic*, Vol. XXVII, No. 8, August 1938, page 404.

48   James Whitcomb Riley Medal: Photograph by Lynn Allyn Young. Collection of Lilly Library, Indiana University, Bloomington, Ind.

48   Great Lakes Medal: Photograph by Lynn Allyn Young. Lynn Allyn Young personal collection

49   Lorado Taft's Studio in the Fine Arts Building: Courtesy of the University of Illinois Archives, ID# 0006088, ca. 1896-1906, found in RS: 26/20/16, Box 30, #121. The holder of this copyright is unknown.

50   Group at luncheon in Lorado Taft's Studio: Courtesy of the University of Illinois Archives, ID# 0005338, ca. 1915-1916, found in RS: 26/20/16, Box 31, #133. The holder of this copyright is unknown.

50   Lorado Taft birthday invitation: Uncredited artwork from collection of Miss Betty Benson

51   Midway Studios and door closeup: Photographs by Lynn Allyn Young. Courtesy of University of Chicago, Chicago, Ill.

52   "Gates" cast: Collection of Miss Betty Benson, probably photographed by Jean Crunelle

53   Proposed Dream Museum: From "Chicago's Historic Museum of Architecture and Sculpture: A World's Fair Suggestion by Lorado Taft," brochure from collection of Miss Betty Benson

54   Lorado Taft and his Dream Museum: Uncredited photograph from Lynn Allyn Young personal collection

54   Fine Arts Building: From "Calumet 412: Forgotten Chicago Ephemera," a blog dated March 13, 2012 calumet412.tumblr.com/post/19238769263/strolling-around-the-art-palace-at-the-columbian

55   Peep Shows: Photos provided courtesy of the Kenosha Public Museum, Kenosha, Wisc.

56   Taft's summer house at Eagle's Nest Colony: Photograph by Lynn Allyn Young. Courtesy of Lorado Taft Field Campus, Northern Illinois University, Oregon, Ill.

57   Taft's original studio: Photograph by Earleen Hinton, *Oregon Republican Reporter*, Vol. 157, No. 17, Oregon, Illinois, April 19, 2007

57   Eagle's Nest cabin: Provided by Jan Stilson, from the Mary Taft Smith albums. Used with permission.

58   "Eternal Indian": Photograph by Lynn Allyn Young. Courtesy of Lowden State Park, State of Illinois

60   Cover of *Scientific American*, September 7, 1912: Uncredited photograph

61   Black Hawk statue construction: Courtesy of the University of Illinois Archives, ID# 0004476, circa 1908-1911, found in RS: 26/20/16, Box 30, Image Number 17. The holder of this copyright is unknown.

61   "Eternal Indian" construction: Courtesy of Beloit College, from the archives of Lewis Williams II, Beloit, Wisc.

62   "Eternal Indian": Photograph by Lynn Allyn Young. Courtesy of Black Hawk Center, Oregon, Ill.

62   Chief Paduke: Photograph by Lynn Allyn Young. Courtesy of City of Paducah, Ky.

62   Union Fountain Indian closeup: Photograph by Lynn Allyn Young. Courtesy of City of Washington, D.C.

63   Proposed Bridge for the Midway in Chicago: Courtesy of the University of Illinois Archives, ID# 0006091, ca. 1909, found in RS: 26/20/16, Box 30, #14. The holder of this copyright is unknown.

64   "Fountain of Creation" figures: Courtesy of the University of Illinois Archives, ID# 0004659, circa 1934, found in RS: 26/20/16, Box 25, Folder Fountain of Creation Negatives Folder 2. The holder of this copyright is unknown.

64   Taft with "Fountain of Creation" model: Wikimedia Commons, from *Chicago Daily News*, 1910

65   Lorado Taft's "Fountain of Creation" model: Courtesy of the University of Illinois Archives, ID# 0006086, before 1918, found in RS: 26/20/16, Box 30, #98. The holder of this copyright is unknown.

66   "Daughters of Pyrrha" and "Sons of Deucalion": Photographs by Lynn Allyn Young. Courtesy of University of Illinois, Urbana-Champaign, Ill.

67-70 "Fountain of Time": Photographs by Lynn Allyn Young. Courtesy of City of Chicago, Ill.

72-73 "Fountain of Time" restoration: Photograph by Andrzej Dajnowski

76   "The Pioneers": Photograph by Lynn Allyn Young. Courtesy of University of Illinois Library, Urbana-Champaign, Ill.

77   "The Pioneers": Photograph by Lynn Allyn Young. Courtesy of City of Elmwood, Ill.

78   Alma Mater being listed by crane, with three workmen: ID# 0000060, August 20, 1962, found in RS 39/2/20, Box CAM-7, Folder CAM 7-1, Alma Mater 1959-62. Copyright *Champaign-Urbana News Gazette*

79   "Alma Mater": Photograph by Lynn Allyn Young. Courtesy of University of Illinois, Urbana-Champaign, Ill.

80   Taft House moving: Courtesy of the University of Illinois Archives, ID# 0002622, November 1981, found in RS: 39/2/20, Box BUI Taft House, Folder BUI Taft House Moving 1981. The holder of this copyright is unknown.

80   Taft House: Photograph by Lynn Allyn Young. Courtesy of University of Illinois, Urbana-Champaign, Ill.

82   "Justice": From "Sculpture at A Century of Progress – Chicago 1933-1934," Edited by Jewett E. Ricker, 3933 Broadway, Chicago

83   "Come Unto Me": Photograph by Lynn Allyn Young. Courtesy of North Shore Baptist Church, Chicago, Ill.

83   Bloch's "Come Unto Me": Courtesy of Beloit College, from the archives of Lewis Williams II, Beloit, Wisc.

84-86 "The Patriots" and "The Pioneers": Photographs by Lynn Allyn Young. Courtesy of the State of Louisiana

87   Lincoln-Douglas debate plaster: Photograph by Lynn Allyn Young. Courtesy of College of Law, University of Ill.

87   Lincoln-Douglas debate bronze: Photograph by Lynn Allyn Young. Courtesy of City of Quincy, Ill.

87   Don Carlos Taft: Photograph by Lynn Allyn Young. Courtesy of Public Library, Elmwood, Ill.

88-89 "Lady Liberty" plaque and Washington, Solomon and Morris Monument: Photograph by Lynn Allyn Young. Courtesy of City of Chicago, Ill.

90   Bulletin of the Krannert Art Museum, cover

91   "The Blind" maquette: Photograph by Lynn Allyn Young. Courtesy of The Oregon Illinois Public Library's Eagles' Nest Art Colony Collection

92   "The Blind" figure group: Photograph by Lynn Allyn Young. Courtesy of the Krannert Art Museum, University of Illinois, Urbana-Champaign, Ill.

92   Candid photo of "The Blind" tableau vivant: Unidentified photographer

93   "Orpheus Consoled": Courtesy of the University of Illinois Archives, ID# 0006084, ca. 1922, found in RS: 26/20/16, Box 30, #44. The holder of this copyright is unknown.

93   Edison Library: Photo provided courtesy of U.S. Department of the Interior, National Park Service, Edison National Historic Site, West Orange, N.J.

94   Mary Ella McGinness memorial: Photograph by Dale Crabtree

94   "Mother and Child" ivorine: Photograph by Lynn Allyn Young. Courtesy of the Lorado Taft Museum, Elmwood, Ill.

95   "Aspiration": Photograph by Lynn Allyn Young. Courtesy of The Oregon Illinois Public Library's Eagles' Nest Art Colony Collection

95   Lorado Taft's Private Studio with figure "Aspiration," Chicago: Courtesy of the University of Illinois Archives, ID# 0006089, ca. 1910s, found in RS: 26/20/16, Box 31, #127. The holder of this copyright is unknown.

96   Travis Ross: Photograph by L. Brian Stauffer, University of Illinois News Bureau, Urbana-Champaign, Ill.

96   Taft gravesite: Photograph by Lynn Allyn Young. Courtesy of Elmwood Township Cemetery, Elmwood, Ill.

98   Young Lorado Taft: Undated photograph by Harris & Ewing, Washington, D.C. Lynn Allyn Young personal collection

126   Lorado Taft on his 76th birthday. Lynn Allyn Young personal collection, from 1936 Associated Press "Wirephoto."

APPENDIX A
Address at Lorado Taft's Funeral

The address that constitutes this appendix was originally published as Charles Clayton Morrison, "Lorado Taft" in *Chicago Theological Seminary Register*, XXVII (January, 1937), 5-8; it is reprinted here with permission.

This address was delivered by Charles Clayton Morrison at the funeral service of Lorado Taft, who passed away on October 30. The service was held in the famous sculptor's studio on the Midway in Chicago. The company and the speaker were gathered at the foot of the towering original plaster cast of the "Fountain of the Great Lakes" from which the bronze statue beside the Art Institute was made. Mr. Taft for many years was chairman of our Seminary's Advisory Board.

Nothing that I can hope to say can add aught to your appreciation of Lorado Taft or your understanding of him. His was one of those rare personalities emerging at infrequent intervals, which, without losing their distinctness as individuals, become, in addition, a kind of Presence. Such men have a pervasive existence. You cannot measure them in terms of biographical data, for they live in our thoughts and in our hearts, not merely as a possession but as a part of ourselves. They have changed the pattern of our minds, and have themselves become apart of the pattern, so that they seem to preside over our tastes and our choices with an authority which is all the more potent for being unintentional and unassumed.

Mr. Taft was such a man. For a half-century he lived and wrought and taught in our midst. Now that he has gone we seem to be more aware of his Presence, and of the unique place he holds in America's cultural community. To define that place is a task which must be left to those who can bring to it an erudition in matters of art which I do not possess. But there are certain human aspects -- shall I call them moral aspects? -- to which I may be permitted to direct your attention.

One of these was the fact that Mr. Taft was, in the finest sense, one of us, and remained one of us throughout his life. He was a native son of Illinois, an alumnus of our state university. The roots of the man were nourished in our midwestern soil, and he seems never to have desired to be transplanted to any other. Mr. Taft's cultural patriotism calls for comment and reflection just because, of all our human interests, I suppose art is the most cosmopolitan. Art at its best is never provincial or nationalistic. Its blossoming times are synchronous with the bursting of bonds and some fresh emancipation of the human spirit. It is right that the artist and the lover of art should seek beauty where its monuments and most abundant and most significant. And there is no disservice to America in confessing the poverty and bareness of our culture in comparison with the riches which Europe has inherited from its glorious past. But it is the human reaction to this confessed fact which marks a distinction among lovers of art. Some react with disillusionment and contempt. Their loyalties cannot endure the comparison, and a kind of cultural expatriation grows up in their thoughts and feelings.

With Mr. Taft it was otherwise. In his younger period he lived for several years in France. He made annual visits throughout his life to the great art centers of Europe, quickening thereby the springs of his own creativity. But he always brought back to his studio in Chicago and to the thousands of students and art lovers all over America who flocked to hear his lectures an enhanced respect not only for the possibilities of art in this country but for the substantial achievements already in evidence here.

This indigenous quality of Mr. Taft's spirit, his firm rootage in a specific cultural soil, expressed itself in his career as a lecturer (his itinerary frequently covered as high as twenty-five thousand miles in a single year), in his devotion to his students, in the constancy of his participation in innumerable local art organizations, as well as in his membership in the learned societies of his peers. But its most characteristic expression was in the annual automobile itinerary covering a week or ten days of visitation to the shrines and the beauty spots of his native state. This unique cavalcade would include forty and fifty and sometimes nearly a hundred persons, not all of them artists in the technical sense, but everyone an art lover and a cultural loyalist.

To make this journey with Mr. Taft was to have one's eyes opened to the great natural beauty of the Illinois landscape, to bring together in a memorable experience the romantic story of the discoverers and pioneers and the actual scene of their adventures. It was conceived both as a pilgrimage to the shrines which now exist and as a search for those sites where, for historical reasons or natural beauty, shrines or monuments could with appropriateness be erected. It was what might be called a field course in historical and artistic appreciation and a course in cultural planning for the future. As the result of these processions there now exists sizable company of like-minded men and women in the larger centers and in the villages of Illinois who participate in a common fund of pride and insight and purpose, constituting a kind of collective intelligence for the guidance of the community's future artistic developments.

I have been speaking of Mr. Taft's unalienated affection for the cultural community in which his life was set, and naturally, layman that I am in matters of art, I tend to seize upon that activity of our great friend which lay outside the technical pursuit of is art. Mr. Taft was a genuine missionary of the gospel of beauty. But of course he was primarily a creative artist. And it is as a creative artist that he reflects most truly his organic integration with his native culture. We are assembled today with the members of his family circle in his workshop. On every side we see his handiwork, together with casts and fragments of great sculpture from the ancient world. We will search in vain through the rooms of this studio for anything which would betoken an interest upon Mr. Taft's part in the modern cult of the uncouth. It may be doubtful taste on my part even to touch the edge of that controversy which divides the judgment of those who have a right to an opinion on what is beautiful and what is ugly, but I mean only to approach near enough to the battle to make one observation concerning Mr. Taft. I would call you to witness that his conscience did not exhaust its function by holding him to the highest degree of faithfulness in the technique of his work. It also functioned in the choice of the subject matter of his art.

It would be presumptuous in me to attempt to interpret Mr. Taft in the complexities of his thought on the question of modernism. And to put forward an opinion of my own in this presence would be an affront. But I think the observation I am making is essentially an ethical one, which I have some right to express, not an esthetic one, concerning which I have no right to speak at all. In rejecting the deformed, the repulsive, and the ugly as the dominant subject matter of his art, Mr. Taft recognized the supremacy of the ethical. His genius as an artist never asserted its superiority to discipline. On the contrary, it found its highest inspiration in the congruity which it discerned between the beautiful and the good. He found his themes, not on the erratic periphery of subjective experience, even if it was his own, but as near the core of social objectivity as possible. From this hard-packed body of social value he broke off the bit that he wanted, transfigured it with his own fresh insight, and made of it a medallion or a bust or a monument.

Here again we have an illustration of the indigenous character of Mr. Taft's personality. It appears not alone in his evangelism but in his instinctive activity as a creative sculptor. He seemed to feel not at all the allurement of the exotic for its own sake, or the subjective for its own sake. These incommunicables did not interest him. His genius ran to the communicable. He had something which he wanted to share. He found no satisfaction in cryptic perverseness. Which only goes to show how integral he was with his cultural environment, how social and objective, and therefore how sound and wholesome was his mind.

If we ran through the list of his great pieces which are scattered like a constellation from Seattle to the capital of the nation, and from Wisconsin to Louisiana, we shall not find one the selection of whose subject matter was not in itself an act of moral dignity and beauty. From the heroic "Blackhawk" at Oregon, Illinois, "The Blind" (inspired by Maeterlinck's play), the "Fountain of the Great Lakes" which stands beside the Art Institute in Chicago, the "Fountain of Time" on Chicago's Midway Plaisance, to "The Sleep of the Flowers" and "The Solitude of the Soul" in the Art Institute -- the list is too long to name more -- one sees a sculptor's genius displaying itself in themes of dignity and elevation and inherent beauty. Yet the selection and treatment of the lofty themes betrayed no moralistic sense of obligation or constraint. The works themselves were a true expression of the kind of man we, his friends, knew Mr. Taft to be. He was following the preachment of the cult of self-expression, but he differed from most followers of that cult in that he had a self that was worth expressing. It would have been impossible for the man we knew to have exercised his genius upon the trivial, ugly or empty deformities which bid for our approval today.

There was a reference which occurred so frequently in Mr. Taft's lectures that it came to stand in my thought as symbolic of his mind and spirit. It was his use of the word "eternal" whenever he undertook to interpret the meaning of art. Naturally, a sculptor whose medium is so much more enduring than the mediums of other arts might think of his work as "relatively" eternal. But this was not Mr. Taft's idea. He meant that the artist, as such, has access to a level of reality which transcends the temporal. The concept of the eternal has been out of date for some time, but I find that it is coming back. The old theological eternal which, taken in stark verbal antithesis to the temporal, offered an escape from this world into another -- that eternal is not likely to return. But what Mr. Taft meant by the eternal is likely to become current not alone among lovers of beauty, but among lovers and worshipers of God. Indeed, I should not be surprised to hear it spoken one of these days on the lips of a psychologist! It is an eternal which is not far away, but here; not mere prolongation of time, the "form" of time, the realm of creative freedom which it is man's highest glory to inhabit.

When I recall in memory the image of Lorado Taft, I see a tall, erect, lithe figure than which another sculptor could find none more admirable in form and bearing and feature to model and cast in bronze. I wonder if such a sculptor could capture that faraway look which seemed to transcend the temporal and to follow the fascinating play of a light that never was on land or sea? I do not know. But to those who were honored by friendship, in however slight a degree, with this great prophet and artist he will always seem as one who saw realities which are hidden from the rest of us not because they are not there but because we do not see.

I think he would like to have us read, while we are assembled here to celebrate his great and fruitful life, these words of Edwin Markham:

> We men of earth have here the stuff
> Of Paradise -- we have enough!
> We need no other stones to build
> The stairs into the Unfulfilled --
> No other ivory for the door --
> No other marble for the floor --
> No other cedar for the beam
> And dome of man's immortal dream.
> Here on the paths of every day --
> Here on the common human way --
> Is all the busy gods would take
> To build a Heaven, to mod and make
> New Edens. Ours the task sublime
> To build eternity in time! [256]

APPENDIX B
Obituary of Allen Weller

Champaign-Urbana News-Gazette, Tuesday, November 18, 1997

A memorial service is planned for Allen Stuart Weller, 90, of Savoy, dean emeritus of the College of Fine and Applied Arts at the University of Illinois.

Mr. Weller, who died Sunday, was dean from 1954 to 1971 and presided over the creation of the Krannert Art Museum and the Krannert Center for the Performing Arts.

During his 17 years as dean, the college more than doubled in size, both in students and staff. It expanded from four to seven teaching departments and from two to four nonteaching divisions. Eight new buildings were added. "He was a great figure," said Maarten van de Guchte, current director of the Krannert Art Museum. "He had a wonderfully rich and wonderfully productive life."

The memorial service will be at a later date. Mittendorf-Calvert Funeral Home, Champaign Chapel, 2400 Galen Drive, C, is handling arrangements.

Mr. Weller died at 6:40 p.m. Sunday (November 16, 1997) at home. He was born Feb. 1, 1907, at Chicago, a son of Harriet Marvin Weller. He married Rachel Fort on Sept. 7, 1929, at Chicago. She survives. Also surviving are a son, John Marvin Weller of Kamloops, British Columbia, Canada; two daughters, Judith Harvey of Greensboro, N.C., and Ruth Khilji of Princeton, N.J.; two grandchildren; and three great-grandchildren. He was preceded in death by two brothers.

Mr. Weller received a bachelor's degree from the University of Chicago in 1927, a master's degree in art history from Princeton University in 1929 and a doctor of philosophy degree from the University of Chicago in 1942.

He was a major in the Army Air Forces during World War II. He served in North Africa and Italy and received the Legion of Merit in 1946.

He taught art history at the University of Missouri from 1929 to 1942 and from 1946 to 1947. Mr. Weller joined the faculty at the University of Illinois in 1947 as a professor of the history of art. He served as head of the Department of Art from 1948 to 1954 before becoming dean of Fine and Applied Arts. He retired as the director of Krannert Art Museum in 1974. "He was very productive up to the last moment of his life," van de Guchte said.

Mr. Weller had just completed work on the book, his second on sculptor Lorado Taft. Titled "Lorado Taft: The Chicago Years," the book will be published by the UI Press.

A tall man, Mr. Weller cut a commanding figure around the college -- ethical, sincere and "with great moral authority, somebody from the old school," van de Guchte said. He regarded Mr. Weller as a valuable mentor. "He was a true encyclopedia of American art. And he had a great sense of the institutional complexities in which the museum has to operate, and was very helpful always with advice," van de Guchte said.

Mr. Weller was confined to a wheelchair in recent years following hip surgery, "but it didn't deter him," van de Guchte said. Harold A. Schultz, professor emeritus of art and design at the University of Illinois, said he had lunch with Mr. Weller at the Krannert Art Museum last Wednesday, part of a series of weekly luncheons that spanned some 40 years. The weekly lunches began with groups of seven or eight individuals from art and design. Eventually, because of retirements and deaths, just Schultz and Mr. Weller kept meeting.
"He was very easy to be with and a joy to have lunch with," Schultz said. "We could talk about everything and anything -- the world of art, politics. He was a philosopher. He was an interesting person because there were so many facets to him." Schultz said Mr. Weller also was a "terrific opera buff." "His interests were wide," he said.

Art and design professor Ted Zernich, former head of the UI School of Art and Design, said Mr. Weller was an "internationally recognized scholar." "He was a very distinguished scholar who elevated the arts at the University of Illinois," said Zernich, who nominated Mr. Weller for an honorary degree in 1993.

Van de Guchte cited Mr. Weller's contributions to the contemporary arts festival held at the UI from 1948 to 1974. "It could not have been possible without Allen Weller's energy, drive and enthusiasm," he said. "Through it, the Krannert Art Museum acquired many outstanding works of art. The museum owes a great deal to his vision." Mr. Weller's friendship with the Krannerts led to their endowments of both the museum and performing arts center, van de Guchte said.

Mr. Weller was also a talented lecturer, delighting audiences with his wit, van de Guchte said. He particularly enjoyed telling stories about donors or famous alumni of the college and "great works of art -- or sometimes not-so-great works of art," he said. "He had a great sense of humor."

Mr. Weller was the Chicago correspondent for Art Digest for six years and the book review editor for the Art Journal for 18 years. He served as vice president and president of the Midwest College Art Conference and was a member of the executive committee of the National Association of Schools of Art and the board of directors of the College Art Association.

He was elected a Benjamin Franklin Fellow of the Royal Society of Arts in London in 1970 and a fellow of the National Association of Schools of Art in 1971. Mr. Weller was one of the original members of the Illinois Arts Council in 1963 and served on the council for 10 years. He served as chairman of the University of Illinois Festival of Contemporary Art from 1954 to 1971.

He received an honorary doctor of fine arts degree from the University of Florida - Gainesville in 1977 and an honorary doctor of human letters degree from the University of Illinois in 1993. He was a member of Phi Kappa Phi and Phi Beta Kappa scholastic honorary societies and Phi Gamma Delta social fraternity.

Memorial contributions may be made to the Ricker Library or Krannert Art Museum.[257]

Reprinted with permission of The News-Gazette, Inc. Permission does not imply endorsement.

APPENDIX C
Obituary of Lewis W. Williams II

Beloit Daily News, Tuesday, August 7, 1990

Lewis W. Williams II, 72, of 1113 Chapin Street, Beloit, died Sunday morning, Aug. 5, 1990, at Beloit Memorial Hospital.

He was born April 24, 1918, the son of Lewis Ward Williams and Ailene Miller Williams in Champaign, Ill. He married Ruth Wininger Dec. 17, 1955, in Champaign, Ill. He was a veteran of World War II, serving with the Air Force.

He was a professor of art at Beloit College from 1955 until his retirement as professor emeritus of the college. During his tenure at the college he received numerous awards and honors, including Teacher of the Year (1966) and a National Endowment for the Humanities grant to participate in a summer seminar on American art and the classical tradition. A noted art historian, he directed the first Beloit College/Associated Colleges of the Midwest London-Florence Seminar 1970-71. He was a frequent speaker at professional meetings, the college's Porter Scholars Program, high school and community groups, and as a guest lecturer at the Milwaukee Public Museum.

Prior to joining the Beloit College faculty, he was on the faculty of the University of Illinois, Northwestern University, and the University of Missouri. He received a Ph.D. in art from the University of Chicago in 1956. He was the author of articles on fine arts and American art and artists, and a distinguished lecturer in the field of art history, especially Far Eastern and Italian Renaissance art. He was a member of the American Association of University Professors.

In addition to his academic career, he was a professional jazz drummer who enjoyed sitting in with local Dixieland jazz bands and was a member of the Musicians Union (ASCAP). He was an honorary member of the National Players Society, a member of the College Art Association, the Beloit Art League, and instrumental in establishing the Beloit Historic Preservation Commission.

Survivors include his wife Ruth; daughter Cynthia Jane (James) McCorkle of Geneva, N.Y.; stepdaughters, Elizabeth Lee (Jeffrey) Roth of Wisconsin Rapids, Wis., and Victoria Anne (Charles) Crawford of Placentia, Calif. and their daughter Laura Crawford; his brother, Frank Williams of Bondville, Ill.; and sister Anna Hedge of Urbana, Ill.

A memorial service will be held Friday, Aug. 10, at 3 p.m. in Eaton Chapel of Beloit College. Interment will be at a later date. Memorials may be made to Beloit College for art books for the Col. Robert Morse Library. Hansen Funeral Home is handling arrangements.[258]

Reprinted with permission of Beloit Daily News, Beloit, Wisconsin.

BUSTS

subject	medium	date	location	confirmed	comments
Baby's Head	terra cotta	ca. 1918	Taft Collection, Krannert Art Museum	yes	in storage; 500 E. Peabody Dr.
Barrows, Rev. John Henry	plaster	1895-96	Taft Collection, Krannert Art Museum	yes	in storage; 500 E. Peabody Dr.
Beldon, Ella Pomeroy	plaster	1895-96	Taft Collection, Krannert Art Museum	yes	in storage; 500 E. Peabody Dr.
Black, John Charles	bronze	1916	Chicago Public Library, Special Collections Room	yes	400 South State Street
Byford, Dr. William H.	bronze	1891, 1895	Galter Health Sciences Libr., Feinberg School of Medicine	yes	303 E. Chicago Avenue, Chicago, Ill.
Bynum, Judge William P.	marble	1915	North Carolina State Library, Raleigh	yes	109 East Jones Street
Campanini, Cleofonte	bronze	1924	Chicago History Museum	yes	in storage; 1601 N. Clark St.
Carpenter, Philo	bronze	1887	Chicago History Museum	yes	in storage; 1601 N. Clark St.
Chamberlin, Prof. Thomas C.	bronze	1915	Geophysical Sciences Building, University of Chicago	yes	5734 S. Ellis, in lobby
Chapin, Pres. A.L.	marble	1897	Wright Art Museum, Beloit College, Beloit, Wisc.	yes	in storage; 700 College St.
Clarkson, Ralph	bronze	1905-06	American Academy of Arts and Letters	yes	633 W. 155 St., New York City
	plaster	1905-06	Taft Collection, Krannert Art Museum	yes	in storage; 500 E. Peabody Dr.
Clendenin, Henry	bronze	1930	Editor's Hall of Fame, University of Illinois	yes	Gregory Hall, 810 S. Wright
Cobb, Silas B.	marble	1894	Cobb Hall, University of Chicago	yes	5811 S. Ellis, in stairwell
Cooley, Thomas McIntyre	bronze	1895	Hutchins Hall, Univ. of Michigan, Ann Arbor	yes	625 S. State Street
Crane, Richard Teller	bronze	1912	Chicago History Museum	yes	in storage; 1601 N. Clark St.
Crerar, John	marble	1891	Crerar Library, University of Chicago	yes	5730 S. Ellis
Culver, E.R.	bronze	1931	Culver Military Academy, Culver, Ind.	yes	in storage; to be housed in the Crisp Visual Arts Center, 1300 Academy Road
Davis, Dr. Ozora S.	marble	1932	Chicago Theological Seminary	yes	58th & University
Eaton, Pres. Edward Dwight	marble	1912	Eaton Chapel, Beloit College, Beloit, Wisc.	yes	College Street, in chapel lobby
Farwell, Sen. Charles B.	marble	1905	Chicago History Museum	yes	in storage, 1601 N. Clark St.
Ficke, C.A.	bronze	1926	Figge Art Museum, Davenport, Iowa	yes	225 W. 2nd St.
Fiske, Horace Spencer	plaster	c.1895	Taft Collection, Krannert Art Museum	yes	in storage; 500 E. Peabody Dr.
Fuller, Henry B.	plaster	1897?	Taft Collection, Krannert Art Museum	yes	in storage; 500 E. Peabody Dr.
Garland, Hamlin	bronze	1895	American Academy of Arts and Letters	yes	633 W. 155 St., New York City
	plaster	1895	Taft Collection, Krannert Art Museum	yes	in storage; 500 E. Peabody Dr.
	plaster	1895	Lakeview Museum (also called "Victorian Gentleman")	yes	1125 W. Lake Ave, Peoria, Ill.
	plaster	1895	Dayton Art Institute	yes	456 Belmonte Park North Dayton, Ohio
Gilbert, Thomas D.	bronze	1896	Veterans' Park, Grand Rapids, Mich.	yes	Library St. and Park Ave.
Girl, Small Bust of	marble head	1885	Taft Collection, Krannert Art Museum	yes	in storage; 500 E. Peabody Dr.
Heckman, Mrs. Wallace	plaster	1905-10	Eagle's Nest Collection, Oregon Public Library	yes	300 Jefferson St., Oregon, Ill.
Jewell, James S.	bronze	unknown	Galter Health Sciences Library, Feinberg School of Med.	yes	303 E. Chicago Avenue
Lawson, Victor	bronze	1930	Editor's Hall of Fame, University of Illinois	yes	Gregory Hall, 810 S. Wright
Logan, Gen. John A.	bronze	1909	Chicago Public Library, Special Collections Room	yes	400 South State Street
Longfellow, H. W.	marble	1907	Main Library, University of Illinois, Urbana	yes	1408 W. Gregory
Loomis, Col. John Mason	bronze	1908	Chicago Public Library, Special Collections Room	yes	400 South State Street
Magoun, Pres. George F.	marble	1890	Grinnell College, Grinnell, Iowa	yes	Goodnow Hall, in lobby
McAll, Robert Whittaker	plaster	1885	Taft Collection, Krannert Art Museum (earliest existing)	yes	in storage ; 500 E. Peabody Dr.

Subject	Material	Date	Collection / Location		Address
Miller, Joaquin	plaster	1898	Taft Collection, Krannert Art Museum	yes	in storage; 500 E. Peabody Dr.
Nixon, Mrs. Charles Eldora	plaster	1898?	Taft Collection, Krannert Art Museum	yes	in storage; 500 E. Peabody Dr.
Northrup, G. W.	bronze	1898	Swift Hall, University of Chicago	yes	1025 E. 58th
Oglesby, Gov. Richard J.	bronze	1907	Chicago Public Library, Special Collections Room	yes	400 South State Street
Pond, Allen B.	plaster	1895?	Taft Collection, Krannert Art Museum	yes	in storage; 500 E. Peabody Dr.
Porter, Prof. William	marble	1893	Wright Art Museum, Beloit College, Beloit, Wisc.	yes	in storage; 700 College St.
	plaster	1893	Taft Collection, Krannert Art Museum	yes	in storage; 500 E. Peabody Dr.
Sherwood, William H.	bronze	1915	Chicago History Museum	yes	1601 N. Clark St.
	bronze	1915	Sherwood Music School-Columbia College Chicago	yes	1312 S. Michigan Ave.
Smith, Mary Taft	plaster	1910-15?	Eagle's Nest Collection, Oregon Public Library	yes	300 Jefferson St., Oregon, Ill.
Studebaker, Mrs. Clement	marble	1929	Studebaker Hall, De Pauw University, Greencastle, Ind.	yes	313 S. Locust St.
Studebaker, Clement	marble	1901	Studebaker Hall, De Pauw University	yes	313 S. Locust St.
Taft, Ada Bartlett, young girl	plaster	1898?	Taft Collection, Krannert Art Museum	yes	in storage; 500 E. Peabody Dr.
Taft, Ada Bartlett	plaster	unknown	Eagle's Nest Collection, Oregon Public Library	yes	300 Jefferson St., Oregon, Ill.
Taft, Don Carlos	bronze	1893, 1936	Morrison and Mary Wiley Library, Elmwood, Illinois	yes	206 W. Main St.
	plaster		Taft Collection, Krannert Art Museum	yes	in storage; 500 E. Peabody Dr.
Willard, Frances E.	marble	1898	Northwestern University Library Archives, Evanston	yes	1970 Campus Drive, Evanston, Ill.
	bronze cast	1931	WCTU Library, Evanston, Illinois	yes	1730 Chicago Avenue
	bronze	1923	Bronx Comm. College Hall of Fame for Great Americans	yes	2183 University Ave.
Williams, Simeon B.	plaster	1886?	Taft Collection, Krannert Art Museum	yes	in storage; 500 E. Peabody Dr.
Zangwill, Israel	plaster	1897?	Taft Collection, Krannert Art Museum	yes	on display; 500 E. Peabody Dr.

PORTRAIT STATUES

Subject	Material	Date	Collection / Location		Address
Cherry, Henry Hardin	bronze	1937	Western Ky. State Teachers Coll., Bowling Green	yes	in front of Cherry Hall, College & 15th streets
Colfax, Schuyler	bronze	1886-87	University Park, Indianapolis, Ind.	yes	Between New York and Vermont streets
Grant, Gen. Ulysses S.	bronze	1889	Historic Fort Leavenworth, Leavenworth, Kans.	yes	Grant and Kearney avenues
Lafayette	bronze	1886	Tippecanoe Cty Courthouse Square, Lafayette, Ind.	yes	301 Main Street
Lincoln, the Young Lawyer	bronze	1927	Carle Park, Urbana, Ill.	yes	Indiana & Garfield
	bronze	1927, 1936	At least five reproductions made; two located at Lincoln Tomb, Springfield, Ill., and the University of Iowa		
	2' bronze repros		records very incomplete		
	plaster reductions		at least fifteen were sold		
	plaster casts of working model		Harper Library (University of Chicago) and Vanderpoel Art Gallery, Beverly, Illinois		
McGinniss, Mary Ella	marble	1889	Crown Hill Cemetery, Indianapolis, Ind.	yes	700 West 38th Street
Porter, Admiral David	bronze	1911	Naval Monument, Vicksburg National Military Park	yes	Vicksburg, Mississippi
Solomon, Haym, Robert Morris and George Washington	bronze	1936, 1941	Wacker Drive at Wabash Avenue, Chicago	yes	northwest corner of intersection
Washington, George	bronze	1909	University of Washington, Seattle	yes	15th Ave NE and NE Campus Parkway
Washington, George	plaster	1909	at least a dozen reductions were sold		

PORTRAIT RELIEFS

Name	Date	Material		Description	Location
Babcock, Stephen Moulton	1934	bronze	yes	Biochemistry Building, Univ. of Wisconsin, Madison	433 Babcock Drive
	1934	dupl. bronze	yes	Stocking Hall, Cornell University, Ithaca, N.Y.	Food Science Dept, 2d fl., Tower and Wing rds.
Custer, General	1889	bronze med.	yes	Michigan Cavalry Brigade Monument	Gettysburg National Military Park, Penn.
Dolliver, Jonathan Prentiss	1925	bronze	yes	Dolliver Memorial State Park, Iowa	2757 Dolliver Park Ave., Lehigh
Douglas, Stephen A.	1902	bronze	yes	Mandel Hall, University of Chicago	1131 E. 57th Street
	ded. 1913	bronze copy	yes	Brandon, Vt.	Rte. 7, in the island next to the Baptist Church
Ferguson, Benjamin F.	1913	bronze	yes	Back of Fountain of the Great Lakes	Art Institute of Chicago, 111 S. Michigan Ave.
Kent, Sidney A.,	1893	bronze tablet	yes	Kent Chemical Laboratory, University of Chicago	1020 E. 58th
Marsh, Charles Allen	1923	bronze	yes	Hyde Park Union Church, Chicago	5600 S. Woodlawn
Porter, W.S. (O. Henry)	1914	bronze	yes	North Carolina State Library, Raleigh	N. Wilmington & E. Jones sts.
Riley, James Whitcomb	1916	bronze medal	yes	500 medals struck by the Medallic Art Society	
Roberts, Bobs	1931	bronze	yes	Comer Children's Hospital, Chicago	in storage; 5721 S. Maryland
Rumsey, Julian S.	unkn.	bronze	yes	Chicago History Museum	in storage; 1601 N. Clark St.
Scovell, Prof. Melville A.	1914	bronze	yes	Kentucky State Agricultural Experiment Station	Scovell Hall, Washington Ave. & S. Limestone, Lexington, Kentucky
Sharp, Katherine Lucinda	1921	bronze	yes	Main Library, University of Illinois	1408 W. Gregory
Stoek, Harry Harkness	1925	bronze	yes	Engineering Library, University of Illinois	1301 W. Springfield Ave.
Westinghouse, George	1915	bronze	yes	Heinz History Center, Pittsburgh, Penn.	in storage. 1212 Smallman Street
Willard, Francis E.	1888	plaster med.	yes	WCTU Rest House, Evanston, Ill.	1730 Chicago Avenue
Willard, Francis E.	1914	bronze	yes	Chanute, Kansas, high school	2012: Contacted school. Plans to donate to local historical society
Willard, Francis E.	1929	bronze	yes	Indiana State Capitol rotunda, Indianapolis	200 W. Washington St.
Willard, Mrs.	1888	plaster med.	yes	Rest Cottage, Evanston, Ill.	1730 Chicago Ave.

OTHER RELIEFS

Name	Date	Material		Description	Location
Bond, Joseph (lettering only)	1928	bronze	yes	Bond Memorial Chapel, University of Chicago	on entryway wall, 1050 E. 59th St.
Come Unto Me	1933	plaster	yes	North Shore Baptist Church, Chicago, Ill.	behind altar, 5244 North Lakewood
Fountain of the Great Lakes	1935	bronze med.	yes	Distributed to members of the Society of Medalists	
Lincoln-Douglas Debate	1936	bronze	yes	Washington Park, Quincy, Ill.	4th & Maine streets
Iroquois Memorial Tablet	1911	bronze	yes	West Entrance, City Hall, Chicago, Ill.	121 N. LaSalle Street
Michigan Monuments	1888-89	stone	yes	Gettysburg National Military Park	Gettysburg National Military Park, Penn.
Spirit of Art (Arche Relief)	1936-37	bronze	yes	Krannert Art Museum, Champaign-Urbana	on display; 500 E. Peabody Dr.

FOUNTAINS

Name	Date	Material		Description	Location
Columbus Mem.Ftn.	1912	marble/gran.	yes	Union Station Plaza, Washington, D.C.	50 Massachusetts Ave. NE
Fountain of Creation	1910-36		yes	4 limestone figures outside University Library and Foellinger Auditorium	University of Illinois, Urbana-Champaign
yes					4 figures in limestone
Fountain of the Great Lakes	1931		yes	Brookgreen Gardens (small figure in bronze)	Brookgreen Garden Dr., Murrells Inlet, SC
	1913		yes	Art Institute gardens, Chicago, Ill.	south of building, 111 S. Michigan Ave.
Fountain of Time	1909-22	cast concrete	yes	Midway Plaisance at Washington Park, Chicago, Ill.	Between 59th and 60th sts., east of Washington Park at Cottage Grove

MONUMENTS & MEMORIALS

Name	Material	Date	Location		Address
Paducah Fountain	Ga. marble	1909	Moved from Courthouse Square, Paducah, Ky.	yes	Now at 19th & Jefferson streets
Thatcher Memorial Fountain	bronze	1918	City Park, Denver, Colo.	yes	Esplanade and 18th Avenue
Trotter Memorial Fountain	Ga. marble	1911	Withers Park, Bloomington, Ill.	yes	E. Washington St. at N. East St.
Alma Mater	bronze	1929	Moved from south of auditorium, University of Illinois	yes	Now at Wright and Green streets, removed for cleaning and restoration 2012
Black Hawk/Eternal Indian	cast concrete	1911	Lowden State Park, Oregon, Ill.	yes	1411 North River Road
	plaster		Eagle's Nest Collection, Oregon Public Library	yes	300 Jefferson Street, Oregon, Ill.
	bronze reproduction		Blackhawk Center, Oregon, Ill.	yes	1101 Jefferson Street
	bronze reproductions		cast for Oregon (Illinois) Trail Days in 2011	yes	
Cavalryman	bronze	1890	Monument Park, Courthouse Square, Warren, Ohio	yes	W. Market St.and Mahoning Ave.
Crusader, The	black granite	1931	Graceland Cemetery, Chicago, Ill.	yes	Clark Street at Irving Park Road
Danville Soldier Monument	bronze/gran.	1922	Danville, Ill.	yes	Gilbert and Main streets
Defense of the Flag, The	bronze	1904	Jackson County Soldiers and Sailors Monument	yes	Washington Park, Jackson, Mich.
	bronze	1894	monument to the Second Minnesota Regiment	yes	Snodgrass Ridge, Chickamauga, Ga.
	bronze	1915	Veterans Cemetery, Marion, Ind.	yes	1700 E. 38th Street
Eternal Silence	bronze	1909	Graceland Cemetery, Chicago, Ill.	yes	Clark Street at Irving Park Road
Hackley, C.H.	bronze	1929	Muskegon (Michigan) High School campus	yes	80 West Southern Avenue
Joliet Soldier Monument	marble/gran.	1889	Courthouse Square, Joliet, Ill.	yes	Will County Courthouse, 14 West Jefferson
Keller, Annie Louise	marble	1929	(flag bearer and possibly lower soldier and sailor) Whiteside Park, White Hall, Ill.	yes	Sherman and Main sts.
Memory (Foote Mem.Angel)	bronze	1923	Woodland Cemetery, Jackson, Mich.	yes	2615 Francis Street
	bronze red.	erected 1938	Taft's grave, Elmwood, Ill.	yes	Elmwood Township Cemetery
Oregon Soldier Monument	marble/gran.	1916	Courthouse Square, Oregon, Ill.	yes	Washington & S. 4th streets
Page, Charles	bronze	1930	City Park, Sand Springs, Okla.	yes	6 East Broadway
Shaler Memorial Angel (Recording Angel)	bronze	1923	Cemetery, Waupun, Wisc.	yes	Madison & Spring streets
	bronze duplicate		Courtyard, Midway Studios, Chicago, Ill.	yes	6016 Ingleside
Soldier Figure	granite	1889	on granite shaft of war memorial, Courthouse Sq.	yes	111 E. Washington St., Morris, Ill.
Winchester Soldier Mon.	bronze	1890-1892	5 bronze figures and relief, Public Square	yes	113 East Washington Street, Winchester, Ind.
Yonkers Soldier Memorial	bronze	1891	4 bronze figures, Philipse Manor Hall, Yonkers, N.Y.	yes	29 Warburton Avenue

FIGURES & GROUPS

Name	Material	Date	Location		Address
Aspiration	bronze	1936	Eagle's Nest Collection, Oregon Public Library	yes	300 S. Jefferson St., Oregon, Ill.
Blind, The	plaster	1907-08	Eagle's Nest Collection, Oregon Public Library	yes	300 S. Jefferson St., Oregon, Ill.
Despair	bronze	1988	Krannert Art Museum, Champaign-Urbana	yes	Kinkead, Pavilion, 500 E. Peabody Dr.
	plaster repro.	1898	Rockford Art Association, Rockford, Ill.	yes	711 N. Main Street
Idyl and Pastoral	marble	1908, 1913	Garfield Park Conservatory, Chicago, Ill.	yes	300 N. Central Park Avenue
Infant Welfare Emblem	bronze	1961	Art Institute of Chicago, Ill.	yes	in storage; 111 S. Michigan Ave.
	ivorine	1914	Taft Museum, Elmwood, Ill.	yes	302 N. Magnolia
Knowledge	plaster repro.	1889, 1902	Rockford Art Museum, Rockford, Ill.	yes	711 N. Main St.

subject	medium	date		location	
Orpheus	bronze	1922	yes	Thomas Edison National Historic Park	211 Main Street, West Orange, N.J.
Patriots and the Pioneers	Ind. limest.	1933	yes	Louisiana State Capitol, Baton Rouge, La.	State Capitol Drive
Pioneers, The	bronze	1928	yes	City Park, Elmwood, Ill.	Central Park N. and Magnolia St.
	plaster	1928	yes	Library, University of Illinois	1408 W. Gregory
	marble	1901, 1914	yes	McCormick Sculpture Court	Art Institute of Chicago, 111 S. Michigan Ave.
Solitude of the Soul, The	plaster	1901		Dayton Art Institute, Dayton, Ohio	456 Belmonte Park North

DIORAMAS

Morning in Florence 1400 (1927)
Donatello's Studio in 1425 (1928)
Nicolo Pisano and Assistants, 1260 (1929-1930)
Phidias' Workshop (1932-1933)
Praxiteles' Studio in 350 BC (1932-33)
Studio of Michelangelo (1934)
Jacapo Della Quercia's Studio 1428 (1935)
Claus Sluter in Dijon (1936-37)

Full diorama sets are located at the Kenosha (Wisc.) Public Museum and at the Museum of Art in Evansville, Indiana (in storage). The set previously owned by the University of Illinois World Heritage Museum was sold at a state auction and is now in anonymous private hands. Individual dioramas are located at the Morrison and Mary Wiley Library in Elmwood, Ill., and at Oregon (Ill.) High School, among other places.

PRESENTLY UNLOCATED WORKS BY LORADO TAFT, last located by Williams in 1958

BUSTS

subject	medium	date	location specified by Williams	comments
Angell, Pres.James Burrill	plaster	1895	Alumni Memorial Hall, Univ. of Michigan, Ann Arbor, Mich.	2012: University of Michigan unable to locate
Barrows, Rev. John Henry	marble	1895-96	Oberlin College, Williams could not locate	2012: Oberlin College unable to locate
Billings, Dr. A.M.	marble	1897	Home of Frank Billings, Lake Forest, Ill.	Location not pursued
Bingham, Ralph B.	bronze	1929	International Platform Assn., Westerville, Ohio	
Cooley, Thomas McIntyre	plaster	1895	Taft Collection	2012: Phone and email search not successful
Davison, Dr. Charles	bronze	1926	University of Illinois Medical School Library	Bust not on Krannert list
Jenny, Major W.B.	plaster	unknown	Taft Collection	2012: Phone and email search not successful
Marlowe, Julia (Mrs. Taber)	plaster	1894	Taft Collection	Bust not on Krannert list
Oliver, James	bronze	1903	Home of Joseph D. Oliver, Jr., South Bend, Ind.	Bust not on Krannert list
	bronze duplicate		Home of Mrs. Gertrude Oliver Cunningham, South Bend, Ind.	Location not pursued
Oglesby, Gov. Richard J.	plaster	1907	Taft Collection	Location not pursued
Oliver, James Doty	bronze	1917	Home of Joseph D. Oliver, Jr., South Bend, Ind.	Bust not on Krannert list
Oliver, James Doty	plaster	1917	Taft Collection	Location not pursued
Root, George F.	plaster	1895?	Chicago History Museum	Bust not on Krannert list
Washington, George	plaster	1909	American Academy of Arts and Letters, NYC	2012: CHM has no record of this piece / 2012: Not at AAAL

PORTRAIT RELIEFS

Buckingham, Everett	bronze	1926	Live Stock Exchange Building, Omaha, Neb.	2012: Phone and email search not successful
Deere, John	bronze	1930	Gymnasium foyer, John Deere High School, East Moline, Ill.	2012: School closed, unable to locate
Delta Tau Delta Memorial	bronze	1920-21	Delta Tau Delta Fraternity, Champaign, Ill. Subjects of the relief are Everette Harshbarger, Ralph Gifford, and Thomas Goodfellow.	2012: Phone and email search not successful
Throop, Amos Gager	plaster med.	1892?	Home of Mrs. Roger T. Vaughan, Homewood, Ill.	Location not pursued

FIGURES & GROUPS

Infant Welfare Emblem	plaster	1914	Taft Collection	Figure not on Krannert list
Despair	plaster	1898	Taft Collection	Figure not on Krannert list
Excelsior	plaster	1884	Taft Collection	Figure not on Krannert list
Knowledge	plaster	1889, 1902	Taft Collection	Figure not on Krannert list
Captain Mollie at the Battle of Monmouth	plaster	1885	Taft Collection	Figure not on Krannert list
Children's Home Society	plaster	1915-16?	Taft Collection	Figure not on Krannert list
Muller, Maud	plaster	1884	Taft Collection	Figure not on Krannert list
Sibyl	plaster	1896	Taft Collection	Figure not on Krannert list

The list of works published in Williams' 1958 dissertation also included known sketches and studies and miscellaneous works, plus unlocated (at that time) busts, portrait statues, portrait reliefs, other reliefs, fountains, figures and groups, sketches and studies, and miscellaneous and commercial works. He also included a list of busts, portrait reliefs, and other reliefs attributed to Taft but assumed to have been created by other sculptors. The entire list is entitled "Part III: Catalogue of the Works of Lorado Taft.[259]

An Associated Press "Wirephoto" from 1936. The caption reads: CHICAGO, APRIL 28 -- SCULPTOR PLANS TO SPEND 76TH BIRTHDAY AT WORK -- Tomorrow is the 76th birthday of Lorado Taft, but he said today he would spend it working on the miniature art gallery for schools he is racing against time to complete. Here he is at his desk working -- not sculpting -- on some of his voluminous correspondence.